From Birth to Seven
Build a Solid Foundation

Carole A. Bell, LPC

From Birth to Seven
Build a Solid Foundation
Copyright © 2016 by Carole A. Bell. All rights reserved.

Cover design by Frank Ball, baby photo by Irina Pommer, older children by Vesna Cvorovic.

Published by:
Bean Hill Press, PO Box 1164, Plainview, TX 79073-1164

Dedication

Because "how we parent" is shared
From generation to generation,
This book is for you:

My parents,
Olan and Allois Alexander,
The greatest gift you gave me
Was your love for each other.

And my children,
Teri Oates Jones and John Oates,
You gave me endless opportunities
To practice my parenting skills
And continue to give me
Great joy.

Acknowledgments

Many people helped me along this journey. Without them, this book never would have happened.

All the students—from little guys to the ones who towered over me—who sat in my offices. They sought my help navigating hard times while they also taught me about kids and families.

My daughter, Teri Jones, who invited me to stay at her home and attend my first North Texas Christian Writers Conference. Her encouragement and her willingness to read and edit through the years have been invaluable.

My husband, Freddy Bell, who encouraged me and supported me financially from the beginning to the end—when finishing the book consumed my life.

My editor, Frank Ball, who gave of himself through North Texas Christian Writers and in an individual editorial relationship. I learned so much about telling a story from his guidance and instruction.

Above all, I acknowledge God's leading through the writing of this book. Without him, I would be nothing but a clanging cymbal.

Table of Contents

Section 1: Beginnings 1

   Your Preschooler as a Teen 2

   Preschoolers and Teens— Is There a Link? 6

   What to Expect in This Book 8

Section 2: Spiritual 9

   Obedience: The Big "O" Word 10

   Quiet Time: Just Between God and Me 19

   Service to Others 26

   Courage: Facing Demons... 35

Section 3: Stewardship 44

   Caring for All God's Gifts to Us 45

   Stewardship in the Closet 53

   God's Ownership... 61

   Blessed to Bless... 69

Section 4: Family 77

   Family United 78

Two Become One.. 89

Section 5: Personal Development 97

Orderliness Tames Chaos................................98

Plan Today for a Smooth Tomorrow 108

Create an Island of Calm in Each Day........................ 118

Section 6: Relationships 126

Between Two Generations 127

Friendships with Peers 136

From Different Planets, but Not So Fast 145

Section 7: Independence............................... 155

That Dreaded Word: Chores................................... 156

Kitchen Lessons 165

My Body: Owner's Manual...................................... 176

Substance Abuse Lessons for Preschoolers.................... 186

Section 8: Endings and New Beginnings 195

Appendix A: Parenting BIG Ideas................................ 197

Appendix B: Communication 101 199

Appendix C: Managing Chore Assignments 201

Appendix D: Discipline and Punishment 204

Appendix E: Volunteer Opportunities for Kids........... 207

Endnotes.. 209

Section 1: Beginnings

We've all found ourselves scanning the rows of books in a store or surfing the web, looking for parenting answers. We settle on one or more books and make our purchases. We try to do what the books say, but we still want to strangle the kid.

I wrote this book because, not only have I been there, but I've listened to countless parents who've traveled the same road.

During these early years, parents lay a foundation, even if they do not make a conscious effort to do so. This book offers tools and techniques to construct the right groundwork.

Built with good materials, a solid foundation will be a lifesaver for the next eighteen years as you prepare to launch your child into adulthood.

Your Preschooler as a Teen

We worry about what a child will become tomorrow,
yet we forget that he is someone today.
Stacia Tauscher

Ethan's Story

The kitchen door banged. Sixteen-year-old Ethan dropped his books on the table and headed to the fridge. "Mom?" He raised his voice. "Mom, do we have any more cheese dip?

Diana walked into the kitchen. "Did you have a good day?"

With one hand on the side of the fridge and the other on the opened door, Ethan looked past the milk and eggs. "Yeah, but I'm starved. I'm looking for the dip."

"Blue dish on the top shelf. How was chemistry?"

Ethan set the dip and a bag of chips on the table and continued to rummage in the fridge. "Okay, I guess. I'm going to shoot hoops with the guys down at the park."

"Not so fast. I got two failure notices today—chemistry and English. Your chemistry teacher says you goof off in class."

Ethan stared at her, eyes narrowed. "That's ridiculous.

"Ethan Maxwell, that's not the way to talk about your teacher. You need to hit the books. The park can wait."

"No. My friends are already there. I'm going to grab a bite and head to the park—now. Chemistry and English can wait."

"Son, I usually leave school stuff to you. But I really think you need to stay here and make a plan for pulling up those grades."

Ethan poured a big glass of milk and looked at his mom as if she had no right to interfere. "Seriously, Mom?"

"Seriously."

Ethan stared at her, waiting for her to back down.

Finally, Diana spoke. "At least stay here long enough to assure me you have a plan."

The muscles in Ethan's jaw twitched as he glared at his mom. He picked up the glass of milk and dumped it down the drain. He shoved the chips and dip across the table. "I'm outta here."

"Ethan, don't leave until we talk about this."

"No, I'm done talking. I'm not staying here listening to you try to control my life. Maybe I'll just flunk the courses and see how you feel about that."

"Don't say that. You'd only hurt yourself."

Ethan picked up his keys, stormed out the door, and enjoyed the long squeal of spinning tires as he drove away.

Why Am I Reading This Book?

If you picked up this book for ideas on raising preschoolers, you must wonder why it begins with a story of a belligerent, disrespectful teen who is flunking two classes. Maybe the next story will provide a clue.

Brianna's Story

On the library floor, Megan sat in the reading circle with her three-year-old daughter, Brianna, on her lap.

The librarian was reading the Dr. Seuss book *Horton and the Kwuggerbug.*[1]

Brianna kicked her heels on the floor.

The boy next to her laughed and did the same thing.

Brianna picked up the pace, looked at her neighbor, and whispered, "Faster."

Megan leaned close to Brianna's ear. "Sugar, be still and listen to the story."

Brianna shrugged away from her mother. "No!" Her voice echoed through the library.

The librarian paused and looked their way.

Megan's heart pounded, and heat crept from the back of her neck around to her face. She rummaged through her purse until she found a stick of gum, which she offered to Brianna as she leaned forward and whispered, "Be quiet and listen, and we'll go for ice cream after story time.

Brianna shook her head. "I don't like this story." She showed no interest in quietly listening.

Silence hung in the room like a giant balloon waiting to explode.

The librarian cleared her throat. Still, no one moved or spoke.

Megan took a ragged breath and thought, *I have to get out of here.* She dumped Brianna off her lap, grabbed her hand in one swift move, and headed toward the door—with Brianna pulling back and protesting the whole way. Her shrill objections echoed like cymbals. Even after they were outside, Brianna was still screaming.

Megan imagined what was now taking place in the reading circle. Probably, after clearing her throat, the librarian took up her book and said, "Well, children, let's see if Horton finds the Beezlenut tree," happy that Brianna's tirade was over.

That Most Embarrassing Moment

Have you ever found yourself in a situation where you had to use physical force to remove your preschooler from the scene? If so, you probably felt your heart racing and blood rushing to your face. Many parents have had this humiliating experience more than once.

A three-year-old's embarrassing and disrespectful behavior can be unnerving. If you're like most moms, all you can think about at that moment is how to control the headstrong preschooler who is causing the scene. You're not thinking about what this child might become—a teen who slams doors, shoves food across the table, and storms out of the house in anger.

Preschoolers and Teens—
Is There a Link?

Direct your children onto the right path,
and when they are older, they will not leave it.
Proverbs 22:6

Preschoolers and teens: the two are connected. The only difference between Brianna's and Ethan's behaviors is that most moms are not in a strong enough position to force the teen to behave.

Some parents think misbehavior in a preschooler is cute. Imagine the four-year-old girl who folds her arms across her chest, sticks out her lower lip, and stomps her foot. When a fourteen-year-old defies authority with that kind of behavior, we're seeing something on the verge of *criminal*, not *cute*.

Can Parents Enjoy Their Teens?

I talk to parents who like their teens. That's right. They tell me they've never had so much fun. Sure, there are bumps in the road, but the teens in their families are responsible soon-to-be adults. They're growing in their relationship with God. They do chores at home, make good grades at school, and treat others with respect and kindness. They're on their way to handling finances, personal care, and relationships—almost ready to leave home and take care of themselves. We describe that healthy condition as "ready to launch." As an added benefit, they laugh together[2] with their families—a vital indicator of healthy relationships.

A Road Map to Age Eighteen

With this book, parents can see down the road to the teen years and learn how the right kind of discipline now will lead their child to a responsible adulthood later.

A trip is much easier when you know your destination. That's why each chapter begins with a set of goals for eighteen-year-olds. Stories and frequently asked questions (FAQ's) illustrate the road markers along the way.

So set your "parenting GPS" for age eighteen. We'll establish the preschool and primary-grade foundations in preparation for what is to come.

What to Expect in This Book

- All guidelines are based on Christian principles.
- Empowerment is a major theme. We should never do for our kids what they can do for themselves. Each chapter includes space for you to record a first step toward empowering your child.
- Discipline is not punishment. Discipline derives from a root word that means "to teach." Punishment is sometimes a part of discipline, but never the whole. (See Appendix D: Discipline and Punishment)
- There will be more stories than instructions.
- All stories are compilations from my thirty-two years in public schools and sixteen years in private practice as a counselor and parenting consultant. No story is from a personal experience with any one individual, even though each one represents a true-to-life situation.
- Online references listed in the Appendices and Endnotes are subject to change. Check my website for the most up-to-date information:
  www.ParentingfromtheSource.com/resources

Section 2: Spiritual

Then the Lord God formed the man from the dust of the ground.
He breathed the breath of life into the man's nostrils,
and the man became a living person.
Genesis 2:7

When God breathed life into us, we became spiritual beings, connected to God through the Spirit. The development of spiritual maturity is the most important, yet most often neglected, responsibility of parenting. We begin there.

Obedience: The Big "O" Word

*The goal of parenting is to produce children who are able
to steward their own freedom.*
Bob Hamp

Goals for Age Eighteen

- Obeys without arguing or procrastinating.
- Obeys people in authority unless they ask for actions
  that violate ethical upbringing.
- Understands the connection between obedience to parents, teachers, and other authority figures and obedience to God.

Ava and the Porcelain Bird

Rachel walked into the family room and found three-year-old
Ava pretend-walking a porcelain bird across the coffee table. "Ava,
that pretty bird is not a toy. It's there so we can enjoy looking at it.
Set it back where it belongs."

Ava held the bird close to her chest, shielding it from her mom.

Rachel pointed to the greenery surrounding a flower arrangement. "Let's pretend this is the bird's nest. He likes to sit right in the middle of it."

Ava stared at the bird as if she were about to lose a friend, then placed him in the greenery. With her arms folded across her chest, she took a deep breath. "I want to hold him."

Rachel pulled Ava onto her lap. "Let's look at him together. What color are his wings?"

Ava unfolded her arms. "Blue."

"If you lean way over, what do you see?" Rachel exaggerated her own efforts to see under the beak. "Can you see the little white spot? It's fun to look at him even if we don't touch him."

Ava bent down to look. "I see it. I *see* it."

"I'll leave it on the table, but you may not touch it. Come and look at it as much as you like. Do you understand?"

Later that day, Rachel found Ava sitting on the floor by the coffee table, holding the bird in her hands.

"Ava, you must not touch or pick up the bird." Rachel took the bird from her and placed it back on the table, knowing she might have to do this more than once, but she was determined to outlast Ava's strong will.

Be Smarter Than Your Child

Even young children are smart enough to figure out how many times it takes for parents to give up enforcing their rules. I think my record for picking up my toddler and putting her back where I told her to stay was twenty-one times—and that was all in the space of a few minutes. After the twenty-first time, she decided I was serious and obeyed.

When one of my kids kept asking to drive before getting his license, I said no over and over and over. In the last month before he was old enough to take his driver's test, he never said a word about driving early. On the big day when he got his license, I asked why he had quit bugging me.

"I quit," he said, "because I decided you were never going to change your mind." It had only taken eight months for him to believe me.

Another trick that children master at a young age is playing for an audience. When you're in a store, in the presence of friends and family or on the phone, they will try what they know is forbidden. They instinctively know it is easier to break a parent's will in the presence of others.

Ava quit picking up the porcelain bird until her grandparents were visiting. While they were watching, she expected her mom to ignore her disobedience.

Mom should never let her get away with this little ploy. Ava must learn that Mom's rules are in force no matter who's watching.

Joseph Likes to Argue

Four-year-old Joseph was playing with his action figures on the family room floor while his mom, Crystal, finished clearing the table after dinner.

She came to the door of the family room. "Joseph, it's nearly time for your bath. Two-minute warning."

Joseph continued to play without giving any indication that he had heard what she said.

Two minutes later, Crystal appeared in the doorway again. "Joseph, time's up. Go."

Again, Joseph didn't look up or move.

Crystal had two choices: (1) Tell him again. (2) Proceed as if she expects him to obey.

Crystal chose the action that would lead to first-time obedience. She walked into the family room and sat by Joseph. "Time's up. You get those three, and I'll carry these. Let's go."

He was slow to respond, so she handed him some toys. "Here, you carry these."

"But Mommy, just a little more time. Please? I'll take my bath really fast."

With most of the toys in her hands, she walked toward the bedroom to put the toys away. She didn't argue with him, because that would have opened the door to negotiation. She'd already told him it was time to go, and he heard her the first time. The issue was settled because she held firm, not allowing Joseph to manipulate her into making it unsettled.

Most kids respond well to a parent who refuses to argue. Joseph followed his mother with the remaining toys in his hands. If he hadn't, she would have picked him up and carried him into the bathroom.

Consistency

Here's good news about demanding first-time obedience. The more you require your child to act without reminders, the easier it gets. Much of parenting is about training ourselves to act in the right way.

Lack of consistency can undo weeks of success in teaching obedience. Let's look at an example in the animal kingdom.

Elsie's Night Out

"Every day, Elsie the cow munched lush grasses across the meadow. Safe and content within the boundaries of barbed wire, she had no thought of going anywhere else. Late one night, headlights pointed her way. Tires squealed as a pickup truck careened off the road, ripped through the barbed wire, and snapped three cedar fence posts, leaving the way open for a midnight tour. The next morning, Farmer Brown swatted her behind, told her to get back to grazing, and repaired the fence. But exploring was much more fun. Several times each day, Elsie checked the mended section of fence, hoping to find a way out."[3]

Our kids do the same thing. If we open the gate just one time, they believe they can persuade us to do it again. Have you noticed that children have an annoying habit of checking the fence again and again—especially in front of other people?

For kids, grownups, or cattle, established boundaries provide empowerment. We all thrive in the meadows because boundaries allow us to relax and make tension-free choices.

Limited Rules

All this talk about obedience may sound like oppressive parenting. It's easier to enforce a few important rules than many less-important ones. Let's take a second look at Ava and that intriguing porcelain bird.

If Ava knows she can touch, pick up, and play with many items in the family room, leaving one item—the bird—untouched will be less painful. I bought a plastic Nativity set that my children were allowed to handle. The others were off-limits. They were okay with that restriction because they had one they could even share with our dog.

FOUNDATIONS FOR THIS STAGE

- Children need to respond when you first tell them to do something. They can say something like "Yes ma'am" or "Okay."
- Consistency makes obedience easier. Tell your child what to do, and always follow through with enforcement.
- Gentle physical intervention, such as picking up the child or removing the toy, may be necessary if she doesn't respond to words.
- Discipline must be enforced even when onlookers are present.
- Early-on, establish the fact that you will not argue. It's nice to have that in place before peer pressure and hormones kick in.

FAQs

When I stand my ground with my child, she throws a temper tantrum. The most recent was in the grocery line, when I wouldn't let her have candy. I was so embarrassed. What should I do when she acts like that?

Ah, those grocery store check-out lines. They are pitfalls for parental embarrassment. Have you noticed how older women stand around with knowing smiles when your child is acting up? Here's a secret: every one of those women, if they're mothers, had a child misbehave in a check-out line. They either dealt with it as I am about to suggest, or they allowed their little darling to use terrorist tactics to get her way. Here is how to handle a tantrum in a store:

While maintaining eye contact, say no once and ask, "Do you understand?" If she has the candy in her hand, tell her in a measured, soft voice to put it back on the shelf.

If she is disobedient after you tell her the first time, take the candy out of her hand and put it on the shelf yourself. Repeat the process as many times as she picks up the candy—until you prevail. Remember that you are setting the groundwork for her obedience when she's a teen.

If she throws a tantrum, turn away and do something else. Visit with the clerk, look through items on the shelf, or unload your basket onto the conveyor.

Stand strong and ignore the knowing smiles of those who are watching. If you feel compelled to respond to their stares, laugh and shrug, saying, "Better now than when she's sixteen."

When you get to the car, do not deal with the issue. Concentrate on your driving, no matter how much she tries to engage you in conversation. Wait until you get home. Silence on the way home will do more to teach her obedience than any kind of lecture.

Once home, address her disobedience without allowing arguments: "Sophia, you know that your behavior in the store was unacceptable. Go to your room and wait for me." She needs to sweat a little, while you decide what you will do. (See Appendix D: Discipline and Punishment.)

My parents say I am too hard on my four-year-old son. I told him to quit playing with his food during a family dinner. He ignored me. I told him a second time and that he would have to leave the table if he did it again. The next thing I see is him trying to push noodles

up his nose. I put the noodles on the plate and helped him out of his chair. As we headed to the bedroom, he wailed, "I want dessert. You promised ice cream for dessert." My dad actually asked if he could take some ice cream to his grandson's bedroom.

Some grandparents are great help in rearing your children. Others, not so much. The best thing is to sit down and talk with your parents about your overall plan for discipline. Explain why teaching obedience is important at this early age. Chances are, your parents disciplined you and have forgotten some of the details.

Becoming a grandparent makes some people lose their bearings, because they love their grandchildren so much. In speaking directly to them, be firm but gentle. Remind them that by requiring obedience now, you are empowering their grandchildren to make good decisions in the future.

Remember that you are the parent. The decision is yours.

PARENT GOALS FOR THIS STAGE

- Strive for consistency. It's hard at first, but it does get easier.
- Keep in mind that you are training for the future. Know that training—whether kids, spouses, or puppy dogs—is much easier when started early.
- Stand strong against intervening family members, friends, and even strangers who might sabotage your discipline plan.
- Even if you have to bite your tongue or put in ear buds, do not engage in an argument with your child.

ACTION TO EMPOWER

I will empower my child by . . .
(describe a boundary you can set that will give your child complete freedom inside that boundary).

_____

_____

_____

_____

_____

_____

Quiet Time: Just Between God and Me

Your word is a lamp to guide my feet and a light for my path.
Psalm 119:105

Goals for Age Eighteen

- Finds immense joy in spending time with God.
- Has an ingrained habit of a daily quiet time.
- Wants to share special time with God for decisions, troubles, and celebrations.
- Identifies resources to aid in understanding God's Word.

Listening to God

Hattie woke early while it was still dark in her grandmother's house. She saw light coming from the living room. Perhaps someone else was up.

She tiptoed down the dark hallway. Her grandmother was sitting in her rocking chair. "What are you doing, Gran?"

"I'm reading my Bible. Come sit with me. I'll read to you."

Hattie crawled into her lap.

Gran wrapped the old quilt around both their shoulders and read from Matthew 18: "If a man has a hundred sheep and one of them wanders away, what will he do? Won't he leave the ninety-nine others on the hills and go out to search for the one that is lost? And if he finds it, I tell you the truth . . ."[4] She read a little longer before she laid her head back and closed her eyes.

"Gran, are you asleep?"

"No."

"What are you doing? Counting sheep?"

"No, I'm listening to God."

"How do you hear him?"

"First, I get quiet and still. Then I think about the words I just read from his Book."

"What did he say?'

Gran raised her head and smiled at Hattie. "Today he said that if any one of us wanders away from being his follower, he'll do everything he can to bring us back to him."

Hattie snuggled deeper into her grandmother's lap. "Read me another story, Gran."

Quiet Time and Prayer before a Child Can Read Independently

Before third grade, most children must work at reading. After that, they begin to read for pleasure. That is why children are often given their own Bibles when they are eight or nine years old.

In the first seven years, the spiritual disciplines are usually parent-directed. Here are some guidelines to make the most of those formative years:

- Start the day with family prayer and Bible reading—over breakfast, if possible. Encourage each child to add to the prayer until he or she is old enough to lead the prayer.
- Schedule a quiet time before "lights out" each night. Using an age-appropriate devotional book, read the suggested scripture and learn to be comfortable with the silence that follows. Our God is polite. He doesn't interrupt us, even when we try to dominate the conversation. The only way we will hear is to close our mouths and open our ears. I wish someone had taught that to me when I was five.
- Pray spontaneously with your children about everything. "Father, calm Jason's tummy. In Jesus' name" or "Lord, that ambulance that just went by may be headed to an accident or someone who is sick. I pray they know your presence at this time."
- Model, model, model. Be the parent whose children expect to find you in your spot with your Bible at the same time every day. Also, let them find you with your eyes closed as you listen to God.
- Encourage a child to begin self-directed spiritual discipline during this developmental stage by saying something like, "Do you remember what Jesus said about forgiving?" or "Why don't you close your eyes so you can hear Jesus and see what he wants you to say to your brother?"

Journaling

I walked into my six-year-old daughter's bedroom where she was playing with Ken, Barbie, and Barbie's BFF, Midge. I was reeling from the pain of a divorce, yet I sought to help my children with their own feelings about "Daddy moving to another house." Therefore, I listened in on their play to know what they were thinking.

I stood in the doorway as the drama unfolded among the three dolls.

Ken (speaks to Barbie): "I decided that I don't want to live here anymore."

Barbie: "But, I want you to."

Ken (walks over to Midge): "Hi, Midge."

Midge: "Hi, Ken."

Ken (kisses Midge): "I like you better than Barbie. Let's go."

Ken and Midge walk away from the scene. Barbie starts to cry.

Their father and I had been careful to protect our children from all divorce discussions. We often met away from our home to talk. I encourage parents to keep adult topics away from little ears, but children will still put bits and pieces together to draw conclusions, which may be fact or fiction.

My daughter, at six, was not old enough to put her thoughts into a nice little bound book called a "journal," but she knew how to express herself through drama.

Before children can write well enough to use writing for expression, encourage them in other artistic forms such as drawing, painting, or sculpting, Drama and music might also be useful. I knew a preschooler who made up "psalms"—his own tunes and words—as he sat in his car seat. His mom turned off the radio because the songs he sang were better.

FOUNDATIONS FOR THIS STAGE

- Quiet time is a necessary discipline if one is to commune with God.
- His Word, the printed Bible, is one way God speaks to us.
- Prayer should be a spontaneous and heart-felt two-way conversation with God.
- Journaling is one way to process our feelings, thoughts, and prayers. When our thoughts are on paper, they do not rattle around in our brains, interfering with our thinking. A few days later, we can read what we've written and be more objective.
- Journaling allows us to reflect on past feelings and measure our progress.
- Before children can comfortably write, they can "journal" through the arts.

FAQs

I'm not even comfortable with my own spiritual disciplines. How can I teach my child?

I wasn't either, and I decided to wait until I had it all figured out. That is one of the biggest regrets of my life.

God esteems our most humble efforts to know him. He will honor our struggles as we learn along with our children. Begin simply. Find an age-appropriate devotional book, read the Scripture, and ask your children, "What is God saying in these words? Does that make you think about anything in your own life?" Remember to let silence prevail after a question. The most important things kids say often follow periods of silence.

Keep in mind that the insights are just between you, your child, and God. The only one of those three who will judge you for your humble effort is you. No one else is looking over your shoulder.

Are there good books to help me with a spiritual discipline plan for my children?

There are great resources, and I will mention some of them. However, the greatest resource is you sitting there with your children, talking about what God seems to be saying in his Word. I know that may be scary, and you might feel inadequate. You're not. God will lead you by his Holy Spirit if you will just step out in faith. However, let me share some resources that will get you started.

- *Draw & Write Journal* from Lakeshore Learning.[5] If your child isn't ready to write, he or she can draw and dictate words for you to write.
- *The One Year Devotions for Preschoolers*[6] by Crystal Bowman and illustrated by Elena Kucharik or *Read and Share Devotional*[7] by Gwen Ellis.
- A Bible appropriate to the age of your child. There are many picture Bibles such as the *Jesus Calling Bible Story Book*[8] by Sara Young and Bibles for beginning readers such as the New International Reader's Version (NIrV)[9].
- *Spiritual Growth of Children*[10] by John Trent. This is a good book about how to have family devotionals and how to lead your children's spiritual growth.
- *Zondervan NIV Nave's Topical Bible*[11]. Look up passages related to subjects that aren't specifically mentioned by name in the Bible. For example, in some versions of Scripture, we don't find the word *school*, but the topical Bible gives many references about teaching children.

- A good study Bible with notes will help you understand historical context and with cross-references to other scripture verses. For instance, when you read Corinthians, you can find references to the verses in Acts about when Paul was in Corinth. Most study Bibles include maps, timelines, and helpful charts.

PARENT GOALS FOR THIS STAGE

- Model the spiritual disciplines of quiet time, prayer, Bible reading, and journaling.
- Establish a routine with your children that includes set-aside times for the spiritual disciplines.
- Allow your children to contribute at the level of their ability.
- Make sure your children have their own age-appropriate Bible.

ACTION TO EMPOWER

I will empower my child by . . .
(list one specific spiritual discipline you will begin and how your child will participate).

_____

_____

_____

_____

_____

Service to Others

Goals for Age Eighteen

- Has experienced a wide variety of service venues.
- Serves alone, with peers and with family.
- Understands the importance of serving others.
- Seeks service opportunities that use his or her own spiritual gifts.
- Finds joy in serving others.

Grandsons Help Deliver Meals on Wheels

Karen smiled at the old lady slumped over in her chair. "Bye now. You have a blessed day."

Mrs. Wilson's was the last house on the route. Karen delivered this Meals-on-Wheels route often, but today she was fortunate to have grandsons, ages four and six, with her. She let them take turns carrying the milk carton while she took the boxed lunch. Between houses, she encouraged her grandsons' questions.

"Why was that lady sad?" the four-year-old asked.

"I think she can't do everything she did when she was younger. She probably can't drive to the store or fix her meals. She may not feel well, because her body is old." Karen noted creases on her grandson's brow. It seemed her answer had not made him feel any better.

"Who helps her?"

Karen put her hand on her grandson's shoulder. "We just helped by bringing a meal. Others bring meals the rest of the week. I bet she has someone who takes her to the doctor and buys what she needs."

"Does she have kids?"

"I don't know. They'd be grownups now."

"Why don't they take care of her?"

"They may help her, but maybe they can't come every day."

Children Are Naturally Compassionate

Some interesting research shows that compassion is a natural response.[12] Children see old people, poor people, and handicapped people the way Christ would want us to see them—as *people* first. Adults often see the condition—age, poverty, or disability—first and then maybe see the person.

We have the opportunity to nurture compassion in our children while they still see with their hearts. We can do that by finding places to serve together as a family.

Many service agencies have age limits that disallow small children. Others make a place for kids who serve with a parent. As you seek places to serve the less fortunate, let your children help make the choices.

Remember that serving others is a way of serving our Lord. Jesus told us that whatever we do for others, we do for him.[13]

An Apple for My Sister

The room filled with people as Hope for Children got underway. These were kids who, without our program, would be at home alone after school. I handed out plastic bags of sliced apples, and the children headed to the tables. Volunteers joined them and assessed their homework needs. As the last child picked up a bag of apples, Maya stood to the side, waiting to speak to me.

"Hi, Maya. Did you get an apple?"

"Yes, Miss."

"Do you need something else?"

She shifted from one foot to the other, hesitating. "Do you have another apple?"

I knelt in front of her. "I do have a few left. Are you extra hungry today?"

"No, Miss. It's not for me. My sister's at home because she's too old to come. She really likes apples, but Mom says they cost too much." Maya seemed to gather her courage and stood a little taller. "May I take her one?"

"How many people live in your home?"

"Three—Rachel, Mom, and me."

"Open your backpack, and let's see what we can do. Can you keep this a secret? I don't have enough extra apples for everyone."

I gathered the remaining apples, about six bags, and stuck them in her backpack. "Your family needs to eat these this evening or tomorrow. After they're cut, they don't keep well. Do you have a refrigerator to put them in tonight?"

"Yes, Miss. But I think we'll eat them for supper."

Many children are compassionate to people outside their family, but less so with siblings, cousins, and friends. That we have a name for the conflict—sibling rivalry—between brothers and sisters tells us how prevalent it is. When sibling rivalry rears its ugly head, the choice to serve becomes difficult.

Why is that? How is the way a child sees her sibling different from how she sees the wounded veteran who is unable to get his newspaper off the driveway? What must we do to cause a heart change toward those who are equals or rivals?

At this age, there are two ways to create a heart change toward equals and rivals (often siblings). We can talk to our children about what it means to be a child of God and how each of us is a child of God, loved by God. We can also teach our children to see into the hearts of others, as addressed in a section below, "Learning to See into Hearts."

Equals and Rivals

The old person who can't go to the store, the wounded veteran who can't go out to get his paper, and even the older sister who is sick in bed on Halloween night are not viewed as equals or rivals. Giving those people a hand up does not cause one's own worth to diminish.

There's a game we play—even as grownups. We look around to see where we stand in relation to others. If we view ourselves as better off in any way, we think it's safe to serve that person. However, if our position is a little shaky because we perceive that we're on the same level or lower, we may not feel confident to risk our position by helping the other person.

A good example of this reaction is the schoolyard bully. Because he feels bad about himself, he picks on others, hoping to bring them down to what he sees as his level.

And by the way, that game we play of assessing our worth compared to others has no value when we see ourselves and others as children of God.

Teaching God's Unconditional Love

From the time children are old enough to listen as you read stories to them, you should be teaching about their worth in the eyes of God. Only when they love themselves will they be able to love others.[14] There are two wonderful story books that I read over and over to my grandchildren. I highly recommend them for teaching how God sees us.

Max Lucado's *You Are Special*[15] tells of a group of wooden people called Wimmicks. All day, they hand out gray dots or gold stars to one another. The pretty and talented Wimmicks get gold stars, and the ones who are not so gifted get gray dots. The protagonist is covered in gray dots until he goes to the Woodcarver and discovers his worth in the eyes of his Creator.

The other book, also by Max Lucado, *If Only I Had a Green Nose*[16], is about the same protagonist who wants to be like everyone else. He follows trend after trend in nose colors (if you're made of wood, a bucket of paint will do the job) until his Creator, the Woodcarver, assures him he is valuable with his original nose.

We often think this lesson is only important to special-needs children who are outwardly different from others. The truth is that every child is acutely aware of his differences, and he needs assurance that he is loved as he is. A child who understands his own worth in God's eyes is set free to serve others.

Learning to See into Hearts

Maya was an exceptional child in that she felt compassion for her sister. Too often, siblings view one another as competition and don't want to extend kindness to them.

But Maya realized that her sister not only missed out on all the fun and help at Hope for Children, but she missed out on an apple snack. One of the traits that helps children develop compassion for others is the ability to see into their hearts. Maya saw into Rachel's heart and wanted to serve her.

As parents, we can help children see from other peoples' viewpoints. One technique is role-playing how the other person might feel. For example, if Maya had not thought to share with her sister, we might say, "Your older sister doesn't get to come here. How do you think she feels about that? Does she have a snack when she gets home from school?"

When we encourage our children to see the other person's point of view, they discover that everyone has needs. Seeing those needs changes their focus.

At this age, considering another person's viewpoint is the beginning of a heart change from focus on *self* to a focus on *others*. The outward focus turns a self-centered child into one who wants to serve—not just the less fortunate, but also those who are equals and rivals striving for attention.

FOUNDATIONS FOR THIS STAGE

- Serving others is a way of serving God.
- Love of self as a child of God is the beginning of love of others. Jesus said, *"Love your neighbor as yourself."*[17] He knew we must love and accept ourselves before we can

31

pour out love to someone else.

- Children tend to feel compassion for those they deem less fortunate than themselves.
- A lifetime of service is best begun at a young age when children see with their hearts.
- Seeing into another person's heart is a way to become compassionate and therefore willing to serve.

FAQs

Both of us work. In the evenings, we're busy with sports, homework, and getting to bed on time. I don't see how we can possibly fit in time to serve others. How can we teach our children this important lesson if there's no time?

Begin with a small commitment. When you and your children make cookies (out of ready-to-bake dough if you are short on time), take some to a neighbor. Pick up groceries for a shut-in while you do your own shopping.

Later, you might choose a bigger commitment such as visiting an adopted grandmother in a nursing home every Saturday morning or buying groceries each week for a housebound neighbor.

See if your church provides volunteer opportunities for kids. Write letters to a service man or woman stationed overseas. Adopt a child in a developing country. Once a month, choose a day for the whole family to pamper one family member.

Sometimes, I look at the people who are getting handouts and think, "Why don't they get a job?" I also worry that I am enabling their poverty by doing something for them. How do I teach my children the right at-

titude about serving?

It helps to serve through an organization that you trust or to serve someone you know, such as a housebound neighbor.

I caution against teaching your children to answer every request for money or services. Instead, teach them to do what they believe God is calling them to do. Even then, there will be times when they help someone who takes advantage of them and the benevolence "system." If the person being served makes poor choices, that's between that person and God. Your children will have done what God asked them to do.

PARENT GOALS FOR THIS STAGE

- Use dialogue that helps your children see another person's point of view—whether siblings or a person you serve, such as a Meals-on-Wheels recipient.
- As a family, find a place to serve the less fortunate on a regular schedule. If possible, do so where the children interact with the recipient.
- Learn to listen while you serve. Most people who receive help have stories to share.
- After you serve with your child, talk about what might be the recipient's viewpoint about life, your service, and his or her limitations.

ACTION TO EMPOWER

I will empower my child by . . .
(give a specific example how your child can help you find the places
or people to serve).

_____

_____

_____

_____

_____

_____

Courage: Facing Demons

I learned that courage was not the absence of fear,
but the triumph over it. The brave man is not
he who does not feel afraid, but he who conquers that fear.
Nelson Mandela

Goals for Age Eighteen

- Knows how to articulate fears.
- Understands that God's Spirit gives the power to be brave.
- Faces difficult challenges with courage.
- Knows the difference between courage and foolish risk-taking.

Come On—You Can Do It

Sophie stood on the edge of the pool, her two-year-old frame trembling. The temperature wasn't what caused the shaking. Fear engulfed her. Her mom, dad, and older brother were in the water, but being from a colder part of the country, she'd never seen a swimming pool before.

Her dad was standing waist-deep in the water in front of her. "Come on. I'll hold you. Sit on the edge and jump into my arms."

"No. I'm scared." She looked to the other side where Mom and Jared were playing. Sophie wanted to be part of the fun, but what she saw was too much water. She wasn't sure about getting in, even with Dad holding her.

"Tell you what, Bugs. Meet me down at that end, and we'll start where it's not so deep." Dad walked up the steps of the shallow end and sat on the edge. "Come sit on my lap and let's put our toes in the water. We won't go any deeper than you want to."

Dad and Sophie sat for a long time with only their feet in the water. They talked about what Mom and Jared were doing and cheered them on in their game of Marco Polo.

"Daddy, let's sit on the step."

"Good idea." Dad slid down until they were sitting in the water.

One small step at a time in the safety of Dad's arms, Sophie conquered her fear of the pool and was soon enjoying the water with her family.

Conquer Fears with Small Steps Close to a Parent

Any new, unfamiliar activity can be frightening to children, but parents can help them overcome those fears. Approach the activity in small steps and stay close to help the child feel safe.

The variety of activities that children fear includes going down a slide at the playground, touching a pet, and leaving a parent to go to a nursery or preschool. Sometimes courage is needed to try a

36

new vegetable that shows up on the dinner plate or to tell the hostess at a birthday party, "Thanks. I had fun." In all these activities, keep in mind that success comes in taking small steps close to a parent. Later, as children gain courage, they can step out on their own and try bigger challenges.

Remember When

Jake was about to begin kindergarten. By checking around, he and his mom learned that none of his friends from preschool would be in his class this year. School started in only a week, and he was fearful.

Jake stared at his bowl of cereal. "I don't want to go to school this year."

Mom sat at the table beside Jake, who had eaten none of his breakfast. "I know you're worried because everyone will be a stranger and everything will be new. I remember a boy two years ago who was afraid to start preschool."

"Who?"

"Well, his name is Jake, and he's sitting at this table with me."

"Ah, Mom. You're silly."

"I may be silly, but it's true you were afraid to start preschool. Do you remember?"

"Kinda."

"After you went into the classroom, I watched from outside the door. Max came over and said hi. Then, before I knew it, you were in the block center with three other children. And some of them became good friends."

"Max is my best friend."

"I know. Do you remember when we talked about courage? We read a story about three young men who refused to worship the king's statue even if it meant being thrown into a fiery furnace.

That was courage. If you hadn't had the courage to go to preschool, you would've missed knowing Max."

Mom pushed Jake's hair out of his face. "You'll see Max on the playground, and he can still come to our house to play. This year, you'll make more friends. I know it's scary, but I want you to be brave and go to kindergarten expecting to make new friends and have a good time."

"Will you go with me?"

"Just like I did two years ago, I'll stand outside the door for a while and watch as you get to know your new friends and teacher. And I'll be waiting after school to hear all about how much fun you had. Now, how about finishing your breakfast? We need to shop for clothes and get your hair cut. We want you to look great on your first day at school."

Recall Past Fears That Were Conquered

Jake is fearful of the unknown. He's comfortable with preschool because he knows what to expect and knows his classmates and teacher. Kindergarten looms as a big unknown, especially since his best friend was assigned to another class.

His mother is wise to talk him through the memory of a previous bout of first-day jitters. She reminds him that he had the same types of fear before, but that turned out well. He met new kids who became good friends. If she continues to use past examples of success to encourage him, each new step will be easier than the last.

One of the keys to having courage today is remembering past moments that required courage and turned out well. God instituted the ritual of Passover for that purpose. Sitting together around the table, the family listens to stories of their history with God. By doing so, they find courage to face the future.

No Spirit of Fear

Mom snuggled Nathaniel and Avery against her as she read to them from *The Children's Illustrated Bible*.[18] The story was one that all kids love. David, a mere shepherd boy, went up against a mighty giant—and won.[19]

Nathaniel leaned forward to look at the picture of David's stone striking down the giant Goliath. "Mom, was David afraid?"

"The Bible doesn't say he was afraid. He didn't sound afraid when we read the story. He got his slingshot and five stones and ran toward the giant. It sounds like he was eager to get into the battle."

Three-year-old Avery looked at her older brother. "I'd be afraid, but I'm not as brave as Nathaniel."

Nathaniel sat up a little straighter. "I'd take a sword, not just a slingshot."

Mom decided it was time to add her thoughts. "Why do you guys think David was so brave? I mean, after all, that was a big giant. Not everyone agrees on how tall he was, but he probably would have to duck to go through doorways."

Nathaniel ran to stand in the doorway. He looked up. "Whoa. That's tall, even taller than Dad."

"And David was probably shorter than I am. So how did he get to be so brave?" Mom made room on the sofa as Nathaniel scooted close to her.

Nathaniel shrugged. "I don't know. How did he?"

"I think the key is in the verse where David says, '*But I'm coming against you in the name of the LORD who rules over all. He is the God of the armies of Israel.*'[20] I think he was brave because he was counting on God's power to work through him. He couldn't have been that brave without God."

Mom leafed through the Bible looking for a verse. "Let me read you another verse that talks about being brave: *God didn't give us a spirit that makes us weak and fearful. He gave us a spirit that gives us pow-er and love. It helps us control ourselves.*[21] Do you know what that means?

Nathaniel hesitated before answering. "Does it mean he doesn't want us to be afraid?"

"That's right. It also says he gives us the power—inside us—to be brave."

"Cool. Avery, you can be brave too."

"Thanks, Nate."

"Nathaniel, you're such a good big brother. Okay kids, it's time for bed. I'll come tuck you in and pray with you. Off you go."

Mom used a favorite story to teach her children that God em-powers them to be brave. She is laying a strong foundation for rely-ing on God in times of fear. That kind of foundation will be im-portant to them when they face greater challenges as young adults.

Is Your Own Fear Affecting Your Child?

Parents should be careful that the fear they see in their child is not actually their own fear. For instance, was I afraid to leave my daughter in the church preschool and let that fear seep into her own feelings? One of the most difficult tasks parents face is that of let-ting go.

While it is good to be cautious with our children, we must trust them to God's protection many times before they're grown. Never let your own fear become their fear.

FOUNDATIONS FOR THIS STAGE

- Children can begin to face fear by taking small steps in the safety of a parent's presence.
- Reviewing past successes in overcoming fears helps children meet new challenges.
- God gives your children a spirit of fearlessness, if they ask. He will work in them to give them courage.

FAQs

My child doesn't want to stay in her class at church while I go to my adult class. When I leave her anyway, I return to find that she cried for me, at least part of the time.

Is this the only place where you leave her? If she's staying without you in a preschool and not here, it would be good to check out what's happening while she is in the class. I suggest eliminating any problem in her class first. Is there a way you can spy? Yes, I said "spy." I did that myself by standing outside the door. I heard what was happening in the class without being seen. When I was satisfied that my daughter was being treated well, I addressed her fear.

Here's a suggestion that may seem a little unorthodox: Have you considered bribery? Long after I was old enough to stay in my Sunday school class without my mom, I cried every time she left. She finally bribed me by telling me that I could make a play suit on the sewing machine if I would stay in class by myself for a whole month. I immediately overcame the fear and was rewarded with a sewing project. No, I'm not going to tell how old I was, but the fact that I made a garment on a sewing machine might give you a clue that I was too old to fear being left alone.

Begin with graduated steps: stay in the room, stay the hallway, and then leave for half the time. That technique follows the guideline of small steps with a parent close by.

My five-year-old child is afraid to talk to strangers who are serving her. For example, we want her to give her order at a fast food counter. Is it wrong to force her to take a step that frightens her?

Begin with an order that she wants, such as ice cream after she's had her meal. You can even have her take a smaller step if you order the ice cream and then turn to your child. "Tell the lady which flavor you want—vanilla or chocolate."

Keep in mind the two guidelines: small steps and your close presence.

It's helpful to practice ahead of time. Role-play the scenario by being the person taking the order while your child practices giving her order. I played "order a hamburger" with one of my children in the park, because the playground equipment had what looked like a drive-in window. It was good that we didn't have to eat all the burgers we "ordered."

PARENT GOALS FOR THIS STAGE

- Examine your own fears to be certain you are not passing those fears to your child.
- Be willing to stay close by as your child faces fears one step at a time.
- Help your child see the relationship between past fears that were overcome and current fears that need to be conquered.

- Using a topical Bible, review stories about others who overcame fear. Read those stories to your children and discuss courage.

ACTION TO EMPOWER

I will empower my child by . . .
(choose a specific fear your child is experiencing and decide on the first small step he or she will take).

_____

_____

_____

_____

_____

_____

Section 3: Stewardship

The earth will not continue to offer its harvest, except
with faithful stewardship. We cannot say we love the land
and then take steps to destroy it for use by future generations.
Pope John Paul II

Stewardship is often used in a limited sense to refer to tithing or taking care of natural resources. It does mean that, but it also means much more. Stewardship is recognizing God's ownership of everything, wanting to return some to him, and using wisely the part we keep.

Caring for All God's Gifts to Us

When someone has been given much, much will be required
in return; and when someone has been entrusted with much,
even more will be required.
Luke 12:48

Goals for Age Eighteen

- Has internalized that God owns everything.
- Returns a portion, not out of obligation, but out of love.
- Understands that stewardship includes care of what God entrusts to us.
- Wants to share with those who have less.

God's Jacket?

Lisa brought some laundry to her six-year-old daughter's room. As she sat on the edge of the bed handing her stacks to put away, she noticed the empty hook where her daughter's jacket belonged. "Julia, where is your jacket?"

Julia looked puzzled. "I don't know."

"Did you wear it home from school?"

"Yes, Mrs. Trevino always makes us get our jackets and back-packs."

"You played outside after you got home. Did you take it off out there?"

"Oh, I remember. I took it off when I was swinging. I left it on the ground."

"It may snow tonight. If your jacket stays outside, what do you think will happen to it?"

"It'd get wet."

"Or Buster might drag it into the doghouse and chew on it. Julia, I want you to learn to take care of things. God has blessed us, but he wants us to be good stewards. Do you remember what *stewards* means?"

"No."

"It means we take care of the things God provides for us to use."

"But *you* paid for my jacket."

"Even though we paid for it, God blessed your dad and me with good jobs so we'd make money. We used some of that money to buy your new jacket."

"What else belongs to God?"

"Actually, everything. And he wants us to take good care of all of it. If your coat gets ruined, we'll have to spend money to buy another one. That's money God might want us to use for something else."

Julia looked at her mom with tears in her eyes. "I'm sorry, Mommy. I won't do it again."

"Come here." Lisa pulled Julia onto her lap. "Let me give you a hug. It's important that you learn to care for your stuff, but you may mess up again. When you do, you're still loved—by God and by me. Now put up this last stack of laundry and run get your jacket."

Honor God and Parents
by Good Stewardship

Lisa is teaching Julia an important concept about stewardship: Everything belongs to God, and he asks us to take good care of it. Even a six-year-old can understand that if she is careless with her possessions and has to replace them, she's spending money that might have been spent for something else.

Another lesson Lisa will teach Julia is that treating her belongings with care is a way of respecting her parents for the money they earn. Although it's God's provision that allows Lisa and her husband to have good jobs, they still get up and go to work every day. They are to be respected for that commitment.

God's ownership can be a difficult concept, both for children and their parents. Lisa is wise to lay a foundation at an early age so she can build on it in the coming years.

The Earth, the Water, the Trees,
and all Creation

A knock on the door was followed by Dad's voice. "May I come in, Son?"

"Sure. Come in, Daddy." At five, Matthew felt grown up when his parents asked permission to enter his room. His dad wasn't smiling. Uh-oh, was he in trouble?

Dad sat on the bed and waited for Matthew to sit by him. "Son,

I just came in from the front yard. The hose was lying in the middle of the yard—running. This is the second time this week that you forgot to turn off the water."

"I'm sorry. I was washing my bike."

"Why do you think it matters to me?"

Matthew tried to remember their conversation just a few days ago. "Because we have to pay for the water?"

"That's true. We do pay for it. We pay for our water by the amount we use. So we'll pay extra for that puddle in the front yard. But there's another reason."

"Umm, I forgot."

"Do you remember in the beginning of the Bible where we read that God created everything? Then God told man to subdue and rule over every created thing.[22] That means God put human beings in charge of all his creation. One way we care for the earth and all that is in it is by not being wasteful. The water running in the front yard was just making a puddle. Because of the recent rains, it's wasted."

Dad put his arm around Matthew. "Do you know some of the ways God wants us to be careful with all he's given to us?"

"By not wasting water. And Grandpa says he plows the ground so the dirt doesn't end up in the next county when the wind blows.

"Right. There are lots of ways we can care for God's creation. You know I like to hunt. I only kill as much as our family can eat. To kill more would be wasteful. Farmers who cut down Christmas trees to sell will plant more trees to grow in their place. There are lots of ways God wants us to be careful with his creation." Dad stood up from the bed. "So Matt, what do you think you need to do right now?"

"Got it, Dad. I'll go turn off the water."

We Are Called to Care for All Creation

Matthew's father is less concerned about the wasted water than he is about teaching his son stewardship. While some people go overboard regarding good stewardship of the earth's resources, it is a Christian foundational concept that we should take good care of the earth and all that is in it.

As Matthew gets older, he will have other opportunities to be a good steward of resources. For example, when he begins to drive, he will want to consolidate trips to save gas, not just for the cost of fuel, but also for the conservation of our resources. At Matthew's young age, Dad is laying a foundation for future understanding of the concept of exercising stewardship by caring for our possessions.

FOUNDATIONS FOR THIS STAGE

- After we give a portion back to God, we're called to take good care of what we keep for our own use.
- Even if we spend money we earned to acquire a possession, it's still by God's provision.
- God's possessions include all of Creation
- Care includes wise use so we don't waste resources.

FAQs

I've always had trouble with the concept that it is God's provision that I make a good living for my family. I work hard. I'm up early to get to work on time. Sometimes staying in bed sounds like a good choice, but I have

to provide for my family, so I get up. How can I give all the credit to God? I need to embrace this concept if I am to teach it to my children. Help!

Thank you for your honesty. Many people feel the way you do and are afraid to admit it.

You are obviously being a good steward of the ability and initiative that God gave you. Evidently, you had some good instruction from parents and teachers along the way. Perhaps God saw to it that you were blessed with opportunities and advantages that otherwise would not have come your way.

One evening before the family meal, a farmer prayed, "God, we plowed the soil, planted the seeds, watered the ground, and pulled the weeds to make the crops grow. Without all that work, we'd have nothing to eat, but we thank you for this food anyway."

If it's difficult to understand God's provision, remember that we didn't create the soil, seeds, and water. God did all that and then gave us the opportunity to "be fruitful and multiply"—a gift of work that adds value to the resources and abilities he provides. Jesus said, "When someone has been given much, much will be required in return,"[23] telling us that what matters is not how much or how little we have, but how well we work with what he has given.

A good exercise to help you recognize God's gifts is to keep a little "Blessings" notebook in which you list the benefits he provides along the way. By writing them on paper, we see them better.

I think there's too much politics involved in caring for our natural resources. I can see both sides of the issue. As a Christian, I want to be on the right side. Where should I stand?

God gave mankind stewardship over all creation: *Then God blessed them, and God said to them, "Be fruitful and multiply; fill the earth and subdue it; have dominion over the fish of the sea, over the birds of the air, and over every living thing that moves on the earth.*[24]

Stewardship is a serious responsibility. Sometimes, we don't do a good job. What we must teach our children—who will be caring for Creation with even more opportunity for misuse than we had—is to always seek God's will apart from special interests.

There must be a balance between man's *use* of Creation and its *preservation*. That balance can only be found by careful search of the Scriptures and prayerful consideration of all sides of the issue.

I have learned about stewardship by living in a farming community where most people want to leave their land in better shape than when they began farming it. At the least, we want to leave the earth in a place of sustainability for future generations as we use our resources for the enhancement of our own lives.

PARENT GOALS FOR THIS STAGE

- Communicate the concept that God is the owner of everything.
- Link wise use of resources to examples that are close to home.
- Introduce the concept that God put the earth and its resources in our care.

ACTION TO EMPOWER

I will empower my child by . . .
(list one way that you and your child will practice good stewardship
of a resource that God has given you).

_____

_____

_____

_____

_____

_____

Stewardship in the Closet

And why worry about your clothing? Look at the lilies of the field and how they grow. They don't work or make their clothing.
Matthew 6:28

Goals for Age Eighteen

- Only buys as many clothes as can be worn.
- Has a system for storage of dirty clothes and knows when to do laundry.
- Is able to sort, wash, and dry clothes.
- Knows the importance of waiting for a full load before washing.
- Folds and hangs clothes so they are accessible.

The Long Row of Jeans

Six-year-old Taylor surveyed her closet as if she were studying a fine painting. She turned to her mom. "I only have three pairs of jeans, and Grace has twelve."

"How did you find that out?"

"When I was at her house, she showed me."

Mom pulled one pair of jeans from the rack and placed it beside the other two. "Do you think you need more?"

"Yes.

"How many more?"

"I don't know."

"Let's think about this. You wear jeans only once or twice a week. You usually wear leggings in the winter. When it's hot, you switch to shorts. It'd be hard to wear twelve pairs many times before you outgrow them. What do you think?"

"I could have a pair with fancy pockets like Grace's and a pink pair. Maybe some other stuff."

"Is there any other reason that you'd like to have twelve pairs?"

"They look cool in her closet."

"Come here, Taylor. Take a good look at your closet. What do you see?"

Taylor laughed as she looked in the closet with her mom. "A mess."

"I have an idea. Let's organize your closet a little better. We'll hang things together so everything looks neat. And while we do that, let's talk about stewardship. Do you remember what that means?"

"That everything belongs to God, and we have to take care of it."

"That's right. And if we spend enough money to buy nine more pairs of jeans, but you hardly wear them before they're too small, would that be good stewardship of the money God provides us?"

"Oh."

"Do you see what I mean? We have enough money to buy twelve pairs of jeans. But we choose to buy fewer. That means we can use the rest of the money for something else."

"But I really want some with fancy pockets."

"As fast as you're growing, you'll soon need new jeans. How about we look at jeans with fancy pockets this weekend? Then we'll know where to find them when you have your next growing spurt."

"Okay."

Mom straightened the last of the clothes on hangers. "And look at your closet now. Dresses are hanging together. Pants are here, tops at the end. Why don't you line up your shoes and put those toys on the shelf? Then you'll have a cool-looking closet."

"Taylor put her shoes in order and picked up some toys. That looks cool. Thanks, Mommy."

Need or Want?

Materialism is an ever-present problem in an affluent society. If we find more jeans that are cute, why not buy them? Then we end up taking jeans to Goodwill, still with tags on them.

Mom is helping Taylor understand that good stewardship includes not buying more clothes than we need. If people do laundry at least once a week, then a week's worth of choices meets their need. Anything above our need is luxury, and that's fine, but to a limited degree.

Taylor's mom also mentioned another concept. Sometimes we tell our children, "We can't *afford* to buy that," when we *actually* choose not to. It's important to teach children that we make choices not to spend money—on clothes as well as other items—even when we can afford it.

Mom is teaching Taylor that she needs to take good care of the clothes she has. In this case, it was simply a matter of organization, which will help Taylor find and wear all her clothes.

But It's Dirty

Five-year-old Jacob came into the kitchen wearing soccer pants, socks, and shoes, but missing his shirt. "Mommy, I can't find my soccer shirt."

"It's time to leave for the game. When did you last see it?"

"I guess at the game."

"That was a week ago. Where did you put it when you took it off?"

Jacob glanced at the ceiling. "I don't remember."

"Well, I didn't see it in the laundry when I washed. But I wasn't looking for it either. You know it's your responsibility to put your things in the hamper. Let's look in your room."

Mom looked in the closet while Jacob looked under the bed. He pulled out the bright green shirt. "Uh-oh."

"Oh, my. Some of last week's snack dribbled down the front. You'll just have to wear it dirty, because it's time to leave."

"I don't want a dirty shirt, Mommy. Coach said it has to be clean."

"Sorry, son. We don't have a choice now. C'mon. We've got to go."

On the way to the field, Mom looked at Jacob in the rear view mirror. "Jacob, I'm sorry your shirt is dirty, but you know you're supposed to put it in the laundry if you want it washed."

Jacob said nothing, still upset that his shirt wasn't clean.

"There's another reason to take care of your clothes," Mom said. "Dad and I have been talking to you about stewardship. God provides your dad with a job to make money for our family. It's our responsibility to be good stewards of the money he makes. That includes taking care of what we buy."

Jacob leaned forward so he could see his mom in the mirror. "Ethan's mom told Coach that she had to buy two shirts because they were always losing one. Can't we do that?"

"Do you think that would be a wise use of the money God provides us?"

Jacob didn't answer.

Mom looked in the mirror and made eye contact. "Jacob?"

"I don't know."

"I think you know the answer. That would be spending extra money just because we didn't want to bother keeping one shirt clean and ready for game day."

Mom pulled into a parking space. "Okay, we're here—and ahead of time. Look at me, Jacob. I love you, and I know you're still learning. Next week will be better. What are you going to do with your shirt when you take it off this afternoon?"

"Put it in the hamper."

"Good deal. Now, give me a high five and get over there with your team."

Learning to Do Laundry Can Begin Early

Learning to keep up with clothes is a hard lesson, but it is easier to teach at five than at fifteen. In addition to putting his dirty clothes in the hamper, Jacob will learn to sort clothes and start a wash.

Doing a load of laundry at five may seem a little early, but Mom can check his sorting and watch as he measures the detergent and chooses the settings. By the time he's eight, he'll be able to wash a couple of loads each week. Not only is that preparing him to take responsibility for his clothes after he leaves home, but your current work load is reduced by his help.

The future may seem a long time away, but teaching a son to do laundry will endear you to a future daughter-in-law.

FOUNDATIONS FOR THIS STAGE

- God wants us to buy the amount of clothes we need and can use.
- A closet full of clothes seldom-worn is poor stewardship.
- Good stewardship includes caring for our clothes.
- Care of clothes includes laundry and storage, even at this early age.
- Both boys and girls need to learn to shop for and take care of clothes.
- A child is empowered by learning laundry skills at this age—unlike a typical teen response of seeing it as a burden.

FAQs

I'm a stay-at-home mom. I see my job as taking care of everything related to our home while my husband works. Soon, my children will be in school. I think we should teach them that school is their job. Asking my kids or my husband to care for their clothes seems like I am abdicating my responsibilities.

I can understand why you think you need to pick up more of the responsibility for the home. However, until your children are in school, caring for and teaching them requires more time than you might realize.

Let's look at several points related to this issue.

Babies, toddlers, and preschoolers require an unbelievable amount of time. By choosing to stay home, you have the opportunity to teach your children during those important years. You may not have thought of it as homeschooling, but that's what you are doing. Important chores like sorting laundry or setting the table are appropriate preschool tasks. The point is that you do not have that much free time if you're "homeschooling" small children.

Also, you are preparing your child for life. If you do not teach your children life tasks while you have them at home, when will they learn? Getting the family involved in chores is not about getting the work done as much as it is making sure that when your eighteen-year-old leaves home, he knows how to take care of himself. He won't learn from your telling him. He must practice.

Finally, don't feel guilty about not working for pay. Most stay-at-home moms are busy for long hours every day. Besides the value of teaching your children how to do jobs, maintaining a home as a "family responsibility" gives each member value. If one person works away from home and the other does menial jobs like scrubbing toilets and getting a meal on the table, an improper hierarchy of job values is easily created. Is this what you want to model for your children? Scrubbing toilets and cooking dinner should both be tasks everyone can do.

I work fulltime. I do well to get the housework and meals done and still get a little sleep. If I slowed down to teach a kid how to do laundry, I'd really get behind. Doing the work myself is easier.

I came home from a late class at the university. After I paid the sitter, I went to my bedroom. In the center of the bed (so I wouldn't miss it) was a stack of my nine-year-old's jeans. On top was a note that said, *I need clean jeans for tomorrow. Thanks.* I had to wash them and get them into the dryer before I went to sleep. I decided it was time to teach laundry skills to both my children.

Extra time was needed to teach them to sort properly, only wash when they had a full load, and take the clothes out of the dryer before they wrinkled. However, the payoff was huge. Before

59

long, they did much of their own laundry and kept track of when they needed something washed. After that initial training, I saved more time than I had invested.

I eased my children into all kinds of chores, confident that when they left home, they could handle being on their own.

PARENT GOALS FOR THIS STAGE

- By the time a child starts school, teach basic laundry sorting and how to wash and dry a load of clothes.
- Set up a system that includes a place to put dirty clothes.
- Organize closet and drawers in a manner accessible to a child.
- Take your child shopping for his or her clothes.
- As you shop, talk to your child about finding the best buys.

ACTION TO EMPOWER

I will empower my child by . . .
(list one chore related to clothing care that you will teach your child).

_____

_____

_____

_____

_____

God's Ownership

Honor the Lord with your wealth and with the best part
of everything you produce.
Proverbs 3:9

Goals for Age Eighteen

- Understands God's ownership of everything.
- Wants to give a portion back to God.
- Understands the concept of caring for the portion we keep.

But I Have to Do the Work

Michelle leaned back and dusted her hands on her jeans. "Wow! We're finished."

Noah counted the hills they had created to plant squash seeds. "One, two, three, four, five. And four tomato plants and six pepper plants. When will the watermelons be ready?"

"Probably in August—right before you start school."

61

Michelle planted a garden every year, but this year, at five years old, Noah had done a lot of the work. "Son, I'm proud of you for sticking it out all afternoon. We've got a great garden. Now all we have to do is water, fertilize, and keep out the weeds. God will do the rest."

"What does God have to do? I'll have to hoe when it's hot. That's hard work."

Michelle turned over the package of leftover squash seeds. "Let's look at what the directions say. The seeds should be planted one inch deep and will need water and sunshine. We can expect to harvest the squash in fifty-five days." She poured one seed into Noah's hand. "God created this seed with a bunch of future squashes programmed into it. He even designed each squash to have seeds that we can plant the next year. He knows how deep the seeds need to be planted and when the squash will be ready for harvest. God also provides sunshine and rain. He knows all this because he created everything, and it still belongs to him."

Noah turned the squash seed over in his hand and then held it to the sunlight.

Mom smiled. "If we save these seeds or the ones from the squash, they all will follow the same plan God designed for them— the need for water and sunshine and the same time to harvest. He didn't do that just for squash seeds, but for everything."

Michelle motioned in a circle around the yard. "God created and provided everything for us. Even if someone puts it together like our picnic table, God provides the raw material."

Noah looked around him. "That's easy out here, but what about inside? Does God own the money that's in my piggy bank? I thought it was mine."

"God loans it for you to use. That's why it's so important for us to ask God how we should use what he gives us.

Michelle stood up and reached for the rake and hoe. "We've done enough work for today. Remember those big juicy lemons we bought at the store yesterday? God grew those, but I bet we can figure out how to make two tall glasses of cold lemonade. How about it?"

Concept of God's Ownership and Provision Is Difficult

Noah struggled with the big concept that God owns everything. He expressed what many of us feel when we put hard work into a project—a feeling of pride in our accomplishment rather than humility before a God who provides.

Even we adults sometimes have a hard time wrapping our minds around those ideas. It's important that children begin early to understand that God not only created but also continues to own it all. When he gives us the responsibility of caring for his creation, we become stewards.

Being a good steward of all that God created and allows us to use will change how we view material possessions. When we understand God's ownership and provision, we have in place an important foundation for a proper relationship with God.

Understanding the Tithe

Three-year-old Allison watched as her mom counted out twenty dimes on the table in front of her. "Allison, your dad and I decided it's time to give you an allowance—money you can use however you want. Help me stack these so that we have ten stacks of two dimes each. Watch." Erin chose two dimes and stacked them on the table. "Like this: I put two dimes in this stack. Now you try it."

Allison arranged dimes until there were ten separate piles. She looked up at her mother as if to say, *Now what?*

"Do you know where this money came from?"

"Your purse."

"Yes, and before that, it was in the bank where your dad and I deposit the pay from our jobs. You've been with me when I put our paychecks in the bank."

Allison shook her blond curls as her face registered amazement. "That's lots of dimes."

"It is, but Dad and I put more than that in the bank, because we want to give some back to God and buy things we need like our home, food, and clothes. Do you know why we give some back to God?"

"He needs it?"

"No, he has everything he needs.[25] All creation belongs to him—the whole earth, our homes, the food we eat—everything. Even these dimes belong to him."

Disappointment flickered across Allison's face. "I thought you were giving them to me."

"I am, because God understands that you need to use some of these dimes for things you want. You can show him thanks by giving back some. In fact, he said one-tenth would be good. That means one of the ten stacks of dimes would be a nice amount to give God."

Erin reached for jars sitting on the table. "Here are three jars. See, one has a cross on it so we know that's what you're giving to God. One has a picture of a bank building because you can save some. The other has your picture on it."

"That looks like our bank."

"It is. I found a picture in an ad."

Mom lined up the three jars in front of Allison. "Now, I want you to do this. Put one stack of dimes in God's jar and one stack in the bank jar."

Allison saw that this was going to be fun. She got up on her knees in the chair and dropped two dimes through the slit in the lid of the tithe jar and two dimes into the savings jar. "Look, Mommy. Look how many are left."

"Let's count them. Can you do that?"

Allison leaned over the table and pointed to each stack. "One, two, three . . ."

She continued until she counted them all. "Eight stacks!" Allison clapped.

"Those eight stacks are the ones that God wants you to use."

"That's a lot!"

"It is a lot. God's very generous. He only asks that we give back a small portion of all he gives us. Giving back is one way we show our love for him."

"And here's the jar with your picture on it. What goes in there?"

"My dimes." With great ceremony, Allison dropped the eight stacks of dimes into her jar.

Visualizing the Concepts

Allison's mom is laying the foundation for the important concept that everything belongs to God, who wants us to return a small portion to him. The stacks of dimes are a visual way of seeing tenths. Labeled jars are useful to store the portions until time to disburse them.

A part of the family's weekly routine will include getting God's portion out of the jar to take to church. Depending on the church, children can place the tithe in a collection plate in the service or in the children's program.

It is important to internalize the concept that we are returning a small portion of the large portion God gives into our care. One way to do that is to develop a habit of taking a tithe to church.

FOUNDATIONS FOR THIS STAGE

- Everything belongs to God, the Creator of all.
- When God put us in charge of caring for his creation, we become stewards.
- We are blessed to be able to give back a portion.

FAQs

This method sounds like a lot of trouble. My mom always handed me a dollar to put in the collection plate. That might even be more money for God. Is it necessary to do the whole "dividing into stacks and putting into jars" routine?

Kids need to see the stacks of coins to get a mental picture of how much they get to keep compared to the small amount they return to God. Piaget[26] called this stage pre-operational, and it lasts until around the age of seven or eight. Until children complete that stage of cognitive development and move into the concrete operational stage, it's impossible for them to understand 10 percent of two one-dollar bills.

It's important for children to set aside their tithe and then place the money in the collection plate. If they have to miss a week, there will be twice as much money to give to God the next time.

This is the beginning of a habit that will bless them throughout their lives. When they get their first real-job paycheck, they will already have the habit of tithing. Hopefully, by then they will use math instead of stacks of money to figure their tithe.

It makes sense to teach our kids to tithe on their allowance just like we tithe on our income. But what about gifts and earnings from extra chores? Should they tithe on that money too?

If Grandma slips your son a few dollars, that is a gift from God channeled through her. Children need to develop an understanding that all money that comes their way is part of God's provision for them.

If you provide your children with opportunities to earn money for chores above their regular responsibilities, they need to tithe on that income too. Extra chores for pay can work well in a family. Children learn skills and work ethics while parents get some jobs done. Children begin with "learner pay" until they can be trusted to do as good a job as someone you would hire. Teach them that God's provision is what gives them the opportunity to earn extra money.

All income is provision from God, and it is an expression of our gratitude to give back to him. Remember that the tithe should always be set aside before any of the money is spent.

Lessons about tithing are best begun at this early age. Children are more receptive than they will be if they first hear about it as a teen.

PARENT GOALS FOR THIS STAGE

- Give allowance in a form that is divisible by ten.
- Talk to your children about God's creation and owner-ship.
- Let children see you write a check for your tithe.

ACTION TO EMPOWER

I will empower my child by . . .
(list one way you will help your child learn to participate in managing his or her tithe).

_____

_____

_____

_____

_____

Blessed to Bless

There is no joy in possession without sharing.
Erasmus

Goals for Age Eighteen

- Wants to share with others.
- Understands that giving often involves sacrifice.
- Connects the concept of stewardship with the sharing of possessions and gifts.

She's Mine

Kate looked up from her computer and ran her fingers through her hair. All afternoon, six-year-old Isabella and five-year-old Sophia had played without arguing. Now, the sound of their voices told Kate that they were locked in a debate over a toy. How would she ever teach them to share?

As she got up, Kate heard Sophia shout, "She's mine. Gran gave her to me for my birthday."

Isabella had an answer—of course. "You've been playing with my gift from Gran all afternoon. You have to share."

"I do not. She's mine."

Isabella's voice took on the temperament of a threat. "I'm telling."

Kate sighed as she walked into their room. "You don't have to tell, Isabella. I can hear. Both of you are shouting."

Kate sat on the floor and motioned for the girls to join her. "Look, girls. There's a better way than shouting. Did you forget why you should share?"

Both girls stared at the floor. Neither spoke.

Isabella looked up with tears in her eyes. "I try to share, Mommy. I let Sophia play in my kitchen all afternoon. I even let her be the boss. She decided what to cook and where we'd eat. I tried to do what you said."

"I know, sweetheart." She looked at Sophia and then back at Isabella. "I am so proud of both of you because you've played for nearly two hours with no fussing. I got lots of work done."

Kate pulled Sophia close to her. "Sophia, tell me about the game you played in Isabella's kitchen."

"We made dinner for company. Isabella cooked tacos and I made Jell-O. We set the table with Isabella's new dishes. She put flowers on the table. Susie and Emma are coming to dinner."

"Why do you think Isabella let you be the one in charge?"

Sophia looked at the ceiling. "Um, because she doesn't like to be the boss?"

"I bet she did it to be nice and share the kitchen and dishes with you."

Sophia leaned closer to Kate but didn't say anything.

"Which one of you remembers what we read in the Bible about sharing?"

Isabella's forehead wrinkled as she tried to remember. "About some people who shared everything?"

70

"That's right. It was the new Christians, and they were starting the church shortly after Jesus went back to Heaven. The Bible says *They didn't claim that anything they had was their own. Instead, they shared everything they owned.*[27] I think the disciples learned to share when Jesus was on the earth with them.

Sophia folded her arms across her chest. "But I do own Emma. Gran gave her to me for my birthday."

"Sweetheart, we talked about how everything belongs to God,[28] and he lets us use it. Gran used money to buy Emma for you, but God made it possible for her to have that money."

Kate pulled both girls closer. "Remember that big word we learned? We are *stewards* of everything God gives us. We take care of it and use it the way he wants us to use it. Do you think God wants you to share Emma with Isabella?"

"I don't know."

"Isabella, what can you do to make sharing easier for Sophia?"

Isabella thought a minute. "I know. Sophia, I'll let you put Susie's new dress on for dinner while I hold Emma."

"Okay." Sophia handed her doll to Isabella.

Sharing Toys

Kate is teaching her daughters about stewardship, which included sharing what God had entrusted to their care. When the girls receive new toys, they're allowed to keep them without sharing for a few days. After that, Kate encourages them to be generous with all their toys.

One way she teaches about sharing is what she did when she asked Isabella how she could make it easier for Sophia. Isabella was accustomed to offering Sophia something to play with while she played with one of Sophia's toys. It is not so much "You have to do something for me if I do something for you." Rather, Kate ap-

71

proaches the situation as "It is nice to find something your sister enjoys while you play with her doll."

Another aspect of God's ownership that was not demonstrated in the story of Isabella and Sophia is that toys are shared with children who have fewer material resources. Kate encourages the girls to clean out their closets twice a year. Older toys are bagged up and delivered to an organization that distributes them to families in need. She emphasizes the idea of God's ownership by reminding them that they enjoyed the toys for a while and can now pass them on to another child God chooses.

Crayons for Owen

"Mom, I need some new crayons for school."

"Oh? Didn't we get you a new box of sixty-four when school started?"

"Well . . ."

Mom stopped chopping onions and turned to face six-year-old Caleb. "We bought a new box a couple of months ago."

"Yes, but . . ."

"Wait a minute. What's going on here? I know you didn't eat them. That was your two-year-old trick."

"Aw, Mom. You know I don't eat crayons anymore. I gave them to Owen."

Mom walked over to the table and sat down. "Come here, Caleb, and tell me what happened."

"I'm sorry, Mom. I guess I should have asked you first, but I was so sad for him. He had a little plastic bag of just a few broken crayons. I saw him looking at my box. So I sneaked them into his desk with a note."

"What did the note say?"

"From a friend."

"Caleb, that's so sweet. Yes, we will get you some more crayons, but I must tell you one thing. If we're going to buy another box of crayons, you'll need to earn some of the money."

"Oh. I didn't know I'd have to do that."

"If they're to be a gift from you, then you must put in some effort to pay for their replacement. You can do that by helping me in the kitchen. I am running behind and still haven't unloaded the dishwasher or set the table. Then after dinner, we'll run to the store for a new box."

"Thanks, Mom. I want to get them tonight so he doesn't find out I gave mine away."

Sacrificial Giving

Caleb's mom is teaching an important lesson. If Caleb can give away his crayons and get a new box with no effort, he's not learning that giving often involves sacrifice. As an adult, there will be times when he must give up something in order to share with someone else.

She was wise in that she made the sacrifice easy enough that it could be done in a short time. At his young age, he probably should not be required to earn the full cost of a new box.

FOUNDATIONS FOR THIS STAGE

- We do not actually "own" anything. All our possessions are on loan from God.
- Jesus teaches us to share with others.
- Giving often requires sacrifice of time or material possessions.

FAQs

It's so complicated to figure out all the rules about sharing. I tend to make rules on the fly to fit the squabble that's happening at that moment. I guess I will feel restricted if I decide in advance how my children must share. Why not just insist that they do what is right and share most of the time?

At this early age, rules are needed to teach your children right from wrong. If they are required—in a loving manner—to share at an early age, it will become a habit that blesses them. They are more likely to share from the heart when they are older, if they practiced sharing early in life. A good rule for parenting is that many rules at a young age means fewer rules in adolescence.

One way to teach sharing is to give children time with a new toy before it is shared. After that, encourage them to let others enjoy their possessions. That makes sense for toys in which you do not want duplicates. For example, you don't need two sets of blocks or two play kitchens. However, the favorite stuffed animal or doll that is a sleeping companion should not have to be shared. You can also decide on a small number of toys that a child doesn't share. As children get older, there will be more possessions that your children control and hence decide when to share.

Many parents have a central location for a toy box. This is a great idea except for the fact that no one is responsible for the toys' care. A little more teaching might be required to get all children committed to caring for shared toys. Establish rules for sharing. For example: a child cannot hang on to one toy while actually playing with a different toy. Children can be creative in their attempts to control several toys. You might need a rule about how long one child can keep a toy. All these variations give you great opportunities to teach what it means to share.

Remember that as you teach sharing, you are also teaching stewardship of possessions. Through God's provision, the toy box overflows. We are called to share our blessings with others.

It seems harsh to make a child earn what he wants to give to someone. After all, his heart is right in wanting to give to his classmate.

If you think about Caleb's situation, until he earns the crayons, he is not the one being generous. When I was a single mom, my children's father often took them shopping and paid for gifts for them to give me. I appreciated the gifts, and the children were excited about giving them. I also was thankful that their father helped them in that way. However, I still have and treasure gifts they bought by pooling their money. It's true, the gifts were not as expensive, but I knew they made a sacrifice to buy them.

It may be necessary to accept some of the expense when children are young. Caleb's generosity should not be discouraged because he can't afford a big box of crayons. At this age, doing some work in exchange for new crayons is enough to teach the concept of sacrificing in order to be generous.

PARENT GOALS FOR THIS STAGE

- Apply the concept of stewardship to your children's toys and other possessions.
- Decide ahead of time whether children will claim exclusive ownership of toys, or whether they will share after a certain amount of time.
- Devise ways that children can participate in the cost of their generosity.

ACTION TO EMPOWER

I will empower my child by . . .
(list one way that you will involve your children in deciding how to share their toys).

_____

_____

_____

_____

_____

_____

Section 4: Family

*A family is a place where principles are hammered
and honed on the anvil of everyday living.*
Chuck Swindoll

Only in family and only in a mere eighteen years do you have the opportunity to prepare your children for the rest of their lives. You hold tremendous power to make the experience amazing or painful, productive or wasted. It's the most important role of any parent, yet it's the one with the least preparation. And it all happens in that small group of diverse people we call family. The good news is that even when we mess up—and we will—God's grace intervenes.

Family United

*A family mission statement is a combined, unified expression
from all family members of what your family is all about—
what it is you really want to do and be—
and the principles you choose to govern your family life.*
Stephen Covey

Goals for Age Eighteen

- Understands and accepts that each family is unique.
- Is loyal to family around other people.
- Seeks the family's company in both times of success and times of failure.
- Contributes to the ongoing refinement of the family's mission statement.

Camping Trips or a New Nintendo?

Six-year-old Jacob plopped down on the couch by his mom. Kim closed her Kindle and patted his knee. "What's up, Jacob?" She pushed back his damp hair. "You've had a workout. Been shooting hoops?"

"Yes ma'am. But Josh just went home. He's got a cool new game system. He always gets the newest one as soon as it comes out."

Kim shook her head. "Son, I'm sorry you feel bad about not having an up-to-date system. I know yours is old. Do the guys make fun of it?"

"Naw. They just say, 'Let's go to Josh's. His Nintendo is new.' They never want to come here."

"Do you remember when we talked about what mattered to our family?"

Jacob laughed. "Yeah, but that was when we were about to go camping. I know camping is way more fun than playing games."

"I get it. It'd help if we went camping every weekend? That'd be perfect, huh?"

Jacob grinned. "Sounds good."

Kim laughed. "When we decided as a family that outdoor stuff was more important, we knew we'd have to give up some things. Having the newest game system is one of them. We even talked about that."

Jacob looked down, hesitating. "I know. I guess I just want everything. It's not fair."

"I understand it's hard, Son, but Dad and I are trying to teach you that we have to make choices. We not only can't have every-thing, we can't do everything—and we shouldn't. By the way, we've talked about letting you and Daniel each take a friend on an overnight camping trip. Would that help?"

A wide grin spread across Jacob's face. "Really? That'd be cool."

"Don't invite anyone yet. We have to talk with Dad and decide on a good time."

"Can we go to Lake Wimberley?"

Kim laughed. "Whoa. Slow down. I tossed that out as an idea, but we need a family council before it's definite." She looked hard at Jacob. "Understand? Before we say anything to friends, we need it calendared."

"Okay." Jacob jumped up from the couch. "Can I tell Daniel?"

"Yes, and tell him it's still a family secret. Listen, camping is super important to our family. We all agree on that. Sometimes friends join us, and sometimes it's just us. But remember, we know we enjoy camping. Seeing someone else's new game system can make us forget. When that happens, just picture me falling in the creek up at White Mountain State Park. I think that was the highlight of the trip for everyone but me."

Jacob patted his mother's arm. "You're a good sport, Mom. I think the best part was when you found some creek varmint in your hair. Your screams woke all the animals in the forest."

Family Character

Kim is teaching Jacob about their family's unique character. Those traits can be a part of its mission statement. Character includes such things as beliefs, interests, and values. Memories, stories, and what makes a family laugh are part of its personality. Putting these attributes on paper can show that their family is one of a kind.

For example, in a family council meeting, Jacob and Daniel's parents asked the boys to talk about all the issues they faced around their peers. One problem was the pressure to have the newest electronics. Instead of *telling* the boys, they let them draw the conclusion that the latest device was soon out of date. Once they had that idea on the table, they were able to make comparisons with other interests the family shared. Their love of the outdoors, camping, and family time came out on top. Camping was recognized as their own special "family hobby." They will reevaluate their choice each year when they review the entire mission statement.

Preparing is Part of the Fun

Camping trips require advance work. The boys always participate with their parents in the planning and preparation. By having responsibilities as they plan a trip, they feel ownership—another part of family character.

If the boys invite friends to join them, Kim will make sure to share contact numbers with the other parents, get a signed release that includes insurance and medical information, and possibly include the other kids in a planning or preparation session.

Brotherly Loyalty around Friends

Dylan shoved his younger brother as they came through the door. "Leave me alone. I don't want to talk to you."

Austin's red face and tear-smeared cheeks said the boys had been fighting again. "I hate you."

Dylan grabbed Austin's backpack as he headed toward his room. "Well, the feeling's mutual, punk."

Lauren stepped between them. "Whoa, guys. Settle down. Come to the kitchen table. Let's get a snack, cool off, and talk about what happened."

Dylan folded his arms across his chest. "I don't want to sit at the table with him."

Lauren took both boys by the shoulders and turned them toward the kitchen. "This is not about what you want, Dylan. I need to know what happened."

The boys sat staring at each other while Lauren poured milk and spread peanut butter.

Silence.

She set snacks in front of them and eased into a chair. "Okay, Austin. You first. Tell me what happened."

Dylan stiffened and glanced at Austin. "Why him? I'm older. I should get to talk first."

"Not today, Dylan. You know we take turns on who talks first after school. "Austin, what happened?"

"First-graders and kinders shared a playground today, and the teachers made us play together. Some older guys were making fun of me because I kept missing the ball." Tears spilled down his cheeks. "Dylan laughed at me. All his friends were laughing, and he stood there and laughed too."

Lauren felt pressure in her chest. *Poor baby.* She reached over and patted Austin's hand, but said nothing. "Dylan, your turn."

Dylan glared at his brother. "It's him. He didn't even *try* to hit the ball. He missed by a mile. Then when the guys started teasing, he cried. What was I supposed to do? Say, 'Way to go, sport'? Then, when we got on the bus, Jackson started teasing him again. All I did, when we got to our street, was say, 'Let's go, punk.'"

Lauren took a deep breath. "Phew. Bad day for both you guys, huh?"

The boys looked surprised and glanced at each other.

Lauren smiled. "Curious why I think you both had a bad day?"

With a bit of hesitation, Dylan and Austin nodded.

"Look guys, a sentence in our mission statement says something about respecting each family member's unique abilities, interests, and personality. Do you remember that? Your dad knows I don't like heights, so he never insists that I help him with a chore if it means I have to climb on the roof—and he certainly doesn't tease me about my fear. We've asked you boys to do the same for each other. That's part of who we are as a family."

82

Austin looked at his brother. "Dylan didn't have a bad day. I did."

Lauren walked to the wall where the framed mission statement hung. "Dylan, come here. I want to show you something."

"Yes ma'am." Dylan pushed back his chair and joined her in front of the document.

Lauren pointed to the bottom of the paper. "What is that right there?"

Dylan looked closely. "My name. It's messy, but I write better than that now."

"That's right. That signature means you agreed to the statement that our family created. You promised to respect your brother, even his differences." As they walked back to the table Mom put her arm around his shoulder. "Tell me how you felt when you were laughing at Austin."

Dylan looked down and said nothing.

"Dylan?"

Still staring at the floor, he mumbled something.

"Let's sit down. And then tell me again how you felt when you laughed at Austin in front of the other kids."

"I . . . I don't know." Dylan looked up with tears in his eyes. "I felt bad."

"Thank you, Dylan, for being honest. So it was a bad day for you too. Now, let's see how your brother felt when you were laughing."

She looked at her younger son. "Austin, I know it's hard, but can you tell Dylan what you thought and how you felt when he joined the others and laughed at you?"

"I felt stupid." Austin wiped tears from his eyes.

Lauren patted Austin's hand. "Thank you, Son. What happened made you feel stupid, and I bet you had another feeling hiding back there. I think you also felt your only hope for someone to stand up for you had just abandoned you. Am I right?"

Barely perceptible, Austin nodded and looked at Dylan.

"Come here, guys. I need a hug from both of you." With one on each side, Lauren enveloped the two boys in hugs. "Okay, we are going to work through the best way to act when something like this happens again. If we plan in advance, the words will come more easily."

Creating and Revising a Mission Statement

Lauren is reinforcing the tenets of their family mission statement. Developed and revised over the previous years, the document represents a compilation of the character of the family and what their values and goals are. When they were first written, they were only words—nice-sounding words. As conflicts and victories came up in the family, the words became part of a living document that helped the boys understand their places and responsibilities in the family.

Writing a mission statement is a big job for a family and can't be done in one evening. I suggest using a spiral notebook to jot down notes over several weeks of around-the-table discussions. Brainstorming opens up new ideas and will help the document evolve. Listed below are some suggested topics to get you started:

- A statement of faith
- Defining values and goals
- Family character or personality
- Things that make your family laugh
- The final authority in your family
- Treatment of each other
- Treatment of each other in the presence of others
- Desired family environment
- Treatment of outsiders and guests
- Ways to handle conflict

These are only suggestions as you begin. Each topic can be written on one page of the spiral notebook as you make notes. Anyone can add ideas during the brainstorming sessions. Later, discuss the ideas until focused, succinct statements define your mission as a family.

Try to keep the statements short. They are more likely to be read and understood if they are to the point. The framed or laminated mission statement should be placed where it can be seen often. Then, as in the story above, use the document to pull the family back to the center when one or more persons are off track. Be open to revision by family council when needed.

FOUNDATIONS FOR THIS STAGE

- A written family mission statement helps a family focus on what's important to the family.
- Family should be a place of jubilant rejoicing over successes, tender encouragement after failures, and gentle correction of wrongdoings.
- Family loyalty is important in the home—and even more so outside the home.
- The uniqueness of a family should be celebrated.
- Members of the family are encouraged to feel good about their own abilities, interests, and physical make-up.

FAQs

I think this all sounds great, but I can't imagine being able to think of all the things that need to be included. I

don't want to develop a statement on the fly—in the heat of an argument or following a gross breaking of (unwritten) rules.

You're right that you shouldn't add to your family mission statement when emotions are involved. At a later time, deal with the issue and address its inclusion in the statement.

For years, I worked for a school district and had a written job description. The last item stated that my job could include any other item assigned by the administrator. That policy didn't always turn out well. But the concept is good. It's wise to include a statement that covers the "uncovered." In my list of ideas above, I have one item that says "The final authority in your family." You might want to clarify with a statement such as the following: It is impossible to foresee all the issues that might not be addressed in this document. For this reason, when a new problem arises, the person/s in charge will make a decision that reflects the overall tone of the document. After the decision is made and the question is resolved, a clarified statement will be brought to family council and included in the document.

The message contains big words for young children, but rather than water down the message, explain the words to the kids. Children have an amazing capacity to learn if someone takes the time to teach.

This "loophole" should be used as little as possible to keep from taking away the power of the document. But it's a good way to remind kids that the parents always have the last word. It's important that if parents invoke their "override" power, the issue is addressed in a family meeting. The decision can be added to the statement as an amendment until it is time to revise.

I'm clueless about how to do this. If I had to list all the rules my two boys might break only in their dealings with each other, the document would go on forever. I al-

so fear pinning myself down. I can imagine one saying, "That's not on the list."

That's why it's important for the list to be general. Let's look at an example that is based on the second story above. Dylan and Austin got off the bus arguing. The issue involved how the older brother had treated his younger brother in front of other kids—how they related to each other outside their home. A general statement endorsed by the family might say: "We will encourage and respect members of our family in the presence of outsiders. If we need to take issue with them, we will do it in the privacy of family." Dylan's behavior toward Austin falls under that statement.

Jesus provided a perfect model for making our mission statement general rather than specific, when an expert in the law questioned him:

"Teacher, which is the most important commandment in the law of Moses?" Jesus replied, "You must love the Lord your God with all your heart, all your soul, and all your mind. This is the first and greatest commandment. A second is equally important: Love your neighbor as yourself. The entire law and all the demands of the prophets are based on these two commandments."[29]

The "law of Moses" referred to includes the Ten Commandments and many more laws found in the first five books of the Old Testament. Yet Jesus expressed them all in two sentences.

A mission statement will be better for being concise. The ideal condition is that a document is so succinct and well-written that it never needs additions. In reality, revision will probably be necessary as the family matures.

PARENT GOALS FOR THIS STAGE

- Discuss with your spouse what you think should be included in a family mission statement. Or if you're a single parent, find a person you can brainstorm with—your parents, a sibling, a trusted friend. Doing this in advance prepares you for discussion with your kids.
- Pray about your vision for your family.
- Search the Internet for examples of family mission statements. Two of the best resources I have found are by Brett and Kate McKay[30] and Focus on the Family.[31] Caution: It's important to create your own as a family rather than copy one from the Internet.
- Plan the brainstorming and family-council sessions in which the mission statement will be developed.

ACTION TO EMPOWER

I will empower my child by . . .
(list one way you will give your child a voice in the creation and implementation of your family's mission statement).

_____

_____

_____

_____

_____

Two Become One

*This explains why a man leaves his father and mother
and is joined to his wife, and the two are united into one.*
Genesis 2:24

Goals for Age Eighteen

- Understands and respects Christian covenant marriage.
- Has seen examples of good marriages in parents, grand-parents, and/or family friends.
- Is prepared to choose a lifelong spouse.

Covenant Marriage Defined

Covenant marriage vows are made to God, to each other, and to the body of Christ. Characteristics of a covenant marriage include unconditional love, sexual purity, and a lifetime commitment. The couple within the marriage grow in relationship with God and each other.

Mommy and Daddy's Date

Four-year-old Grace stood at her mother's elbow, watching her put on makeup. "Mommy, you look pretty."

Crystal smiled at her daughter. "Thank you, sweetheart. Daddy and I have a date tonight." She tucked a blond curl behind Grace's ear. "You look pretty too."

"I want to go on your date."

"Miss Emily is coming to stay with you. The two of you will get to have supper and play games."

Grace scrunched her brows together. "No, I want to go with you."

Crystal laid down her makeup brush and pulled Grace onto her lap. "Sweetheart, there are times when Daddy and I take you and Matt on a family outing. Just last week, we all went to eat at Chipotle and then went to the park. Do you remember?"

"But I want to go with you and Daddy tonight." Grace stuck out her lower lip and crossed her arms.

"Mommy and Daddy need to have time for just the two of us. This is one of those nights. Another time, we'll all go as a family."

Grace climbed off her mother's lap and stomped her foot as she huffed loudly. "That's not fair."

"Grace, this is not about fairness. It's important for Mommy and Daddy to spend time alone together. A date gives us special time to focus on each other. Do you know what marriage means?"

Grace looked down, "I don't know."

"It means we promised God and each other to stay together for the rest of our lives. In order for our marriage to bring us joy, we need time alone."

Crystal pulled a reluctant Grace into a hug. "We also want you to see a good marriage. Then when the day comes that you're getting married, you'll understand why God created marriage."

Crystal held Grace away from her and looked as if she were

90

about to share a secret. "You know what you can do right now? It's only a little while until Miss Emily will be here. Why don't you pick out the game you want to play? Matt's spending the night with a friend. What do you think about that?"

Grace grinned. "It's just girls?"

"That's right. You get Miss Emily all to yourself. You get to choose the games to play and the books to read. No big brother tonight."

Grace hesitated a moment. "I'm going to get Candy Land. Matt never wants to play that."

Children Sense Parents' Bond

From a young age, Grace is learning that there is something special between her parents. Theirs is a relationship that doesn't always include her. At this age, she doesn't understand the reason that she's not allowed to go on their dates. Although she protests, she senses it's okay for her parents to have time alone.

John Wooden, UCLA head basketball coach for twenty-seven years and 1972 Basketball Hall of Fame inductee, summed up this principle when he said, "The best thing a father can do for his children is to love their mother."[32]

Respect for the special bond between parents begins at birth, even if it is not explained with words until later. Small children take note of how their parents greet each other, when they hold hands or hug each other, and how they present a united front when making decisions about their children.

Mommy and Daddy's Bed

Stephanie crawled back into bed.

Robert turned over and struggled awake. "Is she asleep?"

Stephanie pulled up the covers and lay close to Robert. "Finally. I sat on the edge of her bed and rubbed her back until she drifted off."

Robert put his arm around Stephanie and cradled her head against his shoulder. "She's only two. Maybe we should let her sleep in our bed."

Stephanie yawned. "Maybe. That would be the easiest. I keep thinking she'll get used to her own bed soon. If only we hadn't started putting her in our bed."

Robert sighed and pushed Stephanie's hair off her face. "Let's talk about it tomorrow."

"I don't really want her in our bed. I like this better." Her words trailed off as she drifted back to sleep.

Co-Sleeping or Separate Beds?

One of the big debates in parenting circles is over co-sleeping. There are strong points for each side. Those in favor are right that a child enjoys the comfort of having parents nearby. They talk about bonding and security issues. Those opposed point out the dangers of suffocation and the struggle when the time comes for the child to go to a separate bed.

Neither of these groups mention the importance of the sanctity of the marriage bed. Usually those words refer to not having sexual relationships outside of the marriage. In this book, "sanctity of the marriage bed" means the bed parents share is a special place belonging only to them.

Children need to grow up knowing that there is something special between their parents, which excludes them. There is security for children in that knowledge. Especially today, when so many kids come to school talking about their parents' arguments, separations, and divorces, children are comforted when they sense the connection between their parents. One evidence of that bond is that they have a life separate from their children.

The easiest way to keep children in their own beds is to go to their room when they need comforting. When you're dead tired yourself, sitting on the edge of a child's bed until sleep comes may be difficult. But the payoff is big compared to the many sleepless nights of sharing a bed with a small child or trying to break the co-sleeping habit.

FOUNDATIONS FOR THIS STAGE

- During these years, you're laying the foundation for your children to understand the meaning of marriage.
- Marriage is the primary relationship in a family.
- Knowing that their parents have a bond that does not include them is a comfort to children.
- Requiring that children respect the "sanctity" of their parents' bed and bedroom is another way of reinforcing the exclusivity of the parents' relationship.

FAQs

I would love to have our bed to ourselves, but I'm nervous about leaving my two-month-old in another room. I know my husband and I aren't getting the sleep

we need, but I can't imagine not being close in case of an emergency.

There is a compromise between co-sleeping (sharing a bed with your baby) and putting him in a distant room. A bassinet close by gives you peace about a newborn's safety, but allows you to sleep as well as possible. Be sure to move him to his own room soon. With a baby monitor, you will still be able to check on him.

All babies wiggle around, make noise, and wake slightly throughout the night. As new parents, our reaction to that activity is to help them back to sound sleep. When I heard my babies making all that noise, I sneaked into their rooms and jiggled their mattresses because I thought they were waking. What I did was teach them to depend on me to help them go back into deep sleep.

Whether you choose parent-soothing (parent-administered techniques to transition to sleep) or self-soothing (baby/child techniques to transition to sleep), establishing a bedtime routine is important. With a routine, the child receives the signal that it is time to wind down and get ready for sleep. Children who self-soothe learn to go back to sleep on their own after they wake during the night. Dr. Weissbluth's book, *Healthy Sleep Habits, Healthy Child*[33] is an excellent resource for teaching sleep habits. For another perspective on co-sleeping and other issues related to sleeping, visit the website of Dr. William Sears[34] and search for articles on sleep.

The longer you allow your child to sleep in your bed or your room, the harder it will be to make the switch to a separate bed.

I have heard that we should have dates to get away by ourselves. I don't see how we can afford to do that. We're still paying off college loans and struggling to get by without the added expense of dates.

Making a commitment to have a regular date night doesn't have to cost a lot. There are two types of expenses for date nights—child care and entertainment/dining expenses.

The cost of child care can be eliminated by trading with friends. I suggest a token system. If you choose to trade baby-sitting without some system of balancing the time and number of kids, it is easy for friction to develop when one couple overuses the privilege.

A simple way to use tokens is to use one token per kid per hour. If you leave three kids with a friend for four hours that would cost twelve tokens. The couple who does the child care of those three children might want to use the twelve earned tokens for a six-hour afternoon without their two kids. It's a good idea to have three or four couples in the co-op so there's always someone available.

Dates don't have to be expensive. Young couples tell me that some of their most fun dates are cheap or free. Examples include:
- A picnic in the park.
- Coffee and browsing at a bookstore.
- Wandering around the mall.
- Hiking or biking

Someday when you have money for expensive dates, you may discover that they're not as much fun as the "cheap dates" of your early marriage. Rather than just fondly remembering those times, you may decide to try them again.

PARENT GOALS FOR THIS STAGE

- Discuss with your spouse the concept of having a relationship apart from the children.
- Commit to a weekly date. It doesn't have to be expensive. Babysitting can be traded with other couples.
- Decide together how you will handle getting your chil-

95

dren to sleep in their own beds. Once the decision is made, stand united in the face of their protests.

ACTION TO EMPOWER

I will empower my child by . . .
(choose one way your child can participate in date-night plans by planning activities with babysitter).

_____

_____

_____

_____

_____

_____

Section 5: Personal Development

*But until a person can say deeply and honestly, "I am
what I am today because of the choices I made yesterday,"
that person cannot say, "I choose otherwise."*
Stephen R. Covey

There are certain traits of personality that may be called "personal development." They are seldom taught as part of a curriculum. Although some parents do an excellent job of teaching these traits, they often do so by example rather than conscious effort. Knowing how they are little-considered, one might think they are unimportant. However, the child who grows to adulthood without those personal traits will spend a lifetime needing them.

Orderliness Tames Chaos

But be sure that everything is done properly and in order.
I Corinthians 14:40

Goals for Age Eighteen:

- Understands the reason for keeping self and belongings organized.
- Develops own systems for organization.
- Knows how to evolve systems to meet changing needs.

A Place for Everything

Four-year-old Jacob sat among a pile of Legos on the family room floor. He looked up when his mom came into the room. "Mommy, come build with me."

"Oh, honey, I can't right now. We have to clean up before our guests arrive."

"Aw, Mom. Just a *little* while?"

"I'm sorry, Jacob. But you have too many toys in here. Getting everything cleaned up will take some time. Let's get busy."

Jacob tore down his Lego project as only a little boy can do. He was a human wrecking ball making Legos fly every direction.

Melissa handed Jacob a bundle of track pieces. "Whoa, Jacob. I said 'clean up,' not make a bigger mess. Put these away in your room, and I'll bring the cars."

When Melissa went into Jacob's room, she found track pieces scattered in the middle of the floor rather than put away in their plastic box. Jacob was playing with a puzzle he had gotten off the shelf.

"Jacob, what are you doing? I asked you to put away the track. Get their box and pick them up now." She walked over to the shelf to get the box for the cars.

Jacob grabbed the track box and threw in the pieces. "They won't all fit."

"Of course not. Line them up—all going the same direction—and see if that works."

Jacob straightened the tracks and put the box back on the shelf. Then he sat on the floor to work on the puzzle.

Melissa took a deep breath, shook her head, and sat next to him. "Come here, Jacob." She pulled him into her lap. "Let's start over. We need to get all your toys picked up from the family room and put them where they belong. Can you concentrate on that first and then work on the puzzle?"

"Yes ma'am."

"Okay, you need to pick up all the Legos. To do that, you'll need something to put them in. What would that be?"

"Uh, I dunno."

"How about the box that holds Legos? Getting the box will be less work than making several trips with your hands full."

Jacob glanced over at the shelf where the Lego box sat.

"While you get the box and pick up Legos, I'll get the action figures box. After that, we'll each carry a load of books. Then you'll be free to play with the puzzle."

Melissa and Jacob set to work. Cleaning the family room took several minutes. When they finished, Melissa did a high five with Jacob. "Good job. Now, since we have company coming, remember, one toy at a time. What is that rule?"

"I put up one toy before I get out another one."

"That's right."

Organize for Order

Melissa did a great job of organizing Jacob's room in a way that was easy for him to maintain. She purchased inexpensive plastic boxes in a variety of sizes. Because open containers are easier to use, she put away the lids. She bought low shelves. Together, she and Jacob found pictures to label the boxes. As an aid to his future reading, she lettered the names below the pictures.

Jacob does most of his playing in the family room, where he is close to everyone. Melissa encourages him to carry the plastic box to the place he will play, rather than carry some of the contents. That makes it easier to pick up the toys when he's done.

Melissa also puts the clothes he's allowed to choose in the bottom drawers of his chest so he can get them out. Sometimes, he puts away his clean laundry. Melissa is working hard to get him to keep the clothes folded as he puts them in the drawer. Without instruction, he stuffs them in, allowing them to unfold.

At this young age, he likes to put away his clothes. Starting the good habit as a preschooler is much easier than it would be as a teen.

Sorting to Learn Organization

Three-year-old Emily sat at the kitchen table, putting buttons into bowls. (Buttons can be choking hazards. Keep them out of reach of younger siblings.) Amber watched while she prepared the family dinner.

"Mommy, where does this square button go?"

Amber walked over to Emily's sorting project. "Where do you think it goes?"

"Maybe with the big ones, but they're all round. I don't know."

"Oh, now that's a problem. I guess you need to decide if you're sorting by size or by shape. What do you think?"

Emily put her finger by her mouth and looked up.

Amber smiled to herself. *Where did she learn that gesture? Do I do that?*

After a few seconds, Emily looked at the buttons again. "I think I'll sort by size, because I only have one square button."

"Good thinking, Emily. You're right. If you sort by shape, you'll have one bowl with all the round buttons and one bowl with a lonely square button."

Amber returned to dinner preparation while Emily continued her project. When Emily finishes, Amber plans to ask her to sort each bowl of buttons into other bowls for dark and light colors.

Then, Emily will have the pleasure of dumping them all into the fishbowl where Amber keeps her grandmother's button collection. Emily has an impish nature, so she will probably vigorously stir them until there's no evidence of her sorting.

Just yesterday, Emily helped her mother put away clean laundry.

"Emily, which drawer is for socks?"

Emily pulled open the bottom drawer of her chest. "Here!" She picked up a handful of paired clean socks and stuffed them into the drawer.

"Whoa, wait a minute. Let's get those organized."

"Why?"

"In the morning, when you're getting dressed, finding the socks you want will be easier. Let's put the colored socks on the left and the white socks on the right." As Amber explained the system, she sorted socks into the two sides. "Now, I'll let you put the ankle socks in front and the long socks in back."

"I want all the short socks together on this side and all the long socks on the other side."

"That's fine. You're the one using the drawer, so let's do it your way."

Emily set to work. "Look. I don't have colored short socks. They're all white."

"That's okay—short socks on the left and long socks on the right."

Emily carefully arranged each pair of socks in its proper place. When she finished, she beamed at her mom. "See? Is that right?"

"Yes. Good job." She made a fist and Emily quickly responded with a fist bump.

Amber pulled the laundry basket closer. "Now let's see what we can do with the rest of these clothes." She opened the drawer above, and Emily leaned over to look at the stacks of leggings and panties.

Games to Teach Life Skills

Amber uses sorting games to teach organization. There are endless opportunities to teach that skill. Besides buttons, there are cans of food on the pantry shelves, packets of seeds (vegetables and flowers), and picture books.

Besides created opportunities to sort, daily life provides practical opportunities. Emily can sort the clean flatware from the dishwasher before she puts them in the divided drawer. If the rod is low enough for her to reach, she can arrange her hanging clothes by types. Most children have a wide variety of art supplies. Sort them into containers so the wax crayons are not mixed with marking pens.

To make sorting easier, use inexpensive plastic boxes and zippered plastic bags. Even though your child may not yet read, label the containers. Not only does your child learn the importance of reading, but she can learn a few words by constantly seeing them and associating them with the contents. She will understand that words represent things—an important concept needed in formal reading instruction.

Notice that Amber used the words *left* and *right* when talking to Emily about the sides of the drawers. Even though Emily is a little young to learn left and right on her body, she has been introduced to the concept. Amber could even stick a little label inside the drawer, labeling each side as either left or right. Again, she is introducing skills to use, not only in sorting, but also in reading.

One of the most important ways Amber is teaching Emily is by transitioning from games (sorting buttons) to real life (clothes sorted in a drawer). That's an important teaching technique in many areas, because it enables us to hook the child with optional fun games before moving to the necessary skill of keeping her life organized.

FOUNDATIONS FOR THIS STAGE

- Sorting skills are necessary to organization.
- Small children can learn to sort using common objects such as buttons. Sorting skills can be carried into everyday use by organizing socks, other clothes, and toys.

103

- When children take the initiative to devise the sorting system, defer to them. When they "own" the system, they are more likely to use it.
- Having open containers for toys makes organization and cleanup easier.
- Labels, both pictures and words, help children organize and prepare them to read.
- Children should be taught to carry the container to the play area rather than carry part of its contents.
- All these skills will carry over into important functions such as keeping school supplies and books organized.

FAQs

My son is six. I fear that I have waited too long to train him to be organized. His room is a mess. He throws his clothes on the floor rather than putting them in the laundry. Getting him to pick up anything is a major battle. I don't even know where to begin.

No, it's not too late. Anyone can change with the right motivation. And that's the key to change—motivation.

Begin by talking to him. This is not a lecture about his messy habits. Encourage and give him a reason to want order in his life. The conversation might go like this:

"Jason, I've been thinking about your room. You and I both know it's a mess, because we've talked about it. I can see in my imagination what your room would look like if it were organized. When you think of an organized room, what do you see?"

Give him a chance to share his imagined picture. If he acts silly, that's okay. His silliness is because the thought of changing a room he's accustomed to is hard. Ask him again to describe his neat room for you. Begin by giving him the first sentence. "I see a room that has no clothes on the floor. Now you give me an idea."

Explore the reason to be organized. "Yesterday I sent you in here to find your library book, and you couldn't. What if it had been sitting on your desk? Do you think you could have found it? Sometimes you look and look for something until you eventually find it on the floor, under clothes, or under the bed. What would it be like for you to be able to find anything you want?"

Give him a plan. You might say, "I have an idea. Why don't you and I spend some time—maybe two days—getting your room really organized? When we finish, it'll be perfect. Then, we'll figure out how you can keep it that way. Are you game?"

The plan you work out after the room is clean will include some type of monitoring. You can have him check it four times a day. You could check the last of the four times. Reminders could include your asking before he is about to leave or start something new. Eventually, you will want him to monitor himself rather than rely on you. No matter what monitoring system you devise, encourage him to take the lead in planning.

Give him incentive. "When you learn to keep your room neat by yourself, we'll plan a treat for you. You can think about it while you're learning. Maybe a sleepover for a couple of friends? Or the water park will be open soon. We might take your friends there as a reward. We don't have to decide now. Does that sound like a good idea?"

I know this is a long answer, but change is hard. If you have a reason, a plan, and an incentive, change will come more easily. Think about it. We adults are more likely to make permanent changes if we have those three factors in place. The last time you went on a diet, you unconsciously had a reason, a plan, and an incentive.

You asked if it was too late. Believe me, this will be easier at six than at sixteen.

I have a dumping spot in my kitchen that's always a mess. How can I teach my child to keep his room organized when I can't keep that spot neat? Won't he see the hypocrisy of my lessons?

Ouch! Now you're stepping on my toes. I have a dumping spot in my kitchen too. I see two choices of how to handle that.

One: Admit to your child that you have a similar problem, although yours is a spot instead of an entire room. Agree that you will work on changing your habit while he is changing his. You might set up a system of his getting points for "reminding" you to put something away. You will need to handle this carefully since you still want him to act with respect toward you

Two: Decide that we all need a little mess in our lives—with an emphasis on "little." If you choose this route, let him find a spot in his room that can be his dumping ground. He can put down what he brings home from school until he is ready to deal with it. Or he can sling his jacket there until he's ready to detail his room.

With either choice, he is still making great strides toward organization, even if his organization does contain one corner of chaos.

PARENT GOALS FOR THIS STAGE

- Gather bowls and small objects such as buttons to teach your preschooler to sort. Be sure to keep choking hazards away from younger siblings.
- To organize toys, purchase inexpensive plastic containers or be creative and use free containers such as the bottom of milk jugs or other cartons.
- When you organize your child's toys and clothing, have

106

him help you. Explain what you are doing and why.

- Allow your child to devise the system or at least have input.
- Teach and enforce the "one toy at a time" rule.
- Follow through on your instructions to keep toys picked up and sorted in their storage area.

ACTION TO EMPOWER

I will empower my child by . . .
(choose one area to begin organization. Allow your child input on how it needs to be organized).

_____

_____

_____

_____

_____

_____

Plan Today for a Smooth Tomorrow

Before anything else, preparation is the key to success.
Alexander Graham Bell

Goals for Age Eighteen

- Understands the importance of preparing for tasks in advance.
- Takes a few minutes at the end of each day to assess the needs of the next day.
- Applies daily preparedness techniques to long-term goals.

After-School Download

Jill watched out the door as Braden stepped off the school bus. He waved goodbye to friends and ran home. Jill stepped back, so he wouldn't know she was watching. She admitted it: she was overprotective. After all, the bus dropped him off a half block away, and he was only a kindergartner.

When Braden burst into the house, she was busy getting a snack ready. She tried to make the coming-home time special for the two of them. They always sat at the table, ate a snack, and re-hashed the day.

Braden came into the kitchen. "Hi, Mom. I'm home."

"Hey, Braden. How was school?"

Braden slid into the chair and eyed the plateful of raw veggies and bowl of hummus. "Yuck. I want chips, not veggies."

"No. It's veggies today. How was school?"

"Okay, I guess. Ava got sick in class and threw up in the door-way."

"Poor Ava and poor class until it got cleaned up."

"Yeah, it was stinky. She went to the nurse's office and left us with the mess. We had to step over it to go to music."

Jill laughed. "Tell me something good."

Braden's face lit up. "The teacher liked my story. She had me read it to the class."

"Braden, good job."

Braden and Jill visited a few more minutes while he ate all the hummus and a few of the veggies. Jill treasured their time together each afternoon.

She took the dishes to the counter. "Okay, let's look over your school stuff."

Braden opened his backpack and pulled out the folder his teacher used to communicate with parents. "Here's my check list. Five smiley faces and one frown."

"I'm proud of you for getting five smiles. Wow! And especially the one for staying in your seat. That's been hard to learn, huh?" Jill gave Braden a high five.

She pointed to the one frown. "What were you doing instead of paying attention?"

"I was bored. I was thinking about riding my scooter."

"Okay, what do you need to do tomorrow to get a smiley face for paying attention?"

"I can do it, Mom. I just forgot."

"Okay. I'm counting on you." Jill pulled a paper out of the folder. "What's this?"

"We have a field trip next week."

"Okay, let's put it on your calendar."

Braden dug in his bag until he found the small spiral assignment book. He set it on the table between them.

"The note says the field trip is next Friday the tenth. Let's see if you can find April tenth in here."

Braden found April with no trouble, because Jill had had him paper-clip all the past weeks together. He turned until he found the page that included *10 Friday*. "Here it is" He beamed as he handed the book to his mom.

"Okay, Braden. What are we putting on the tenth?"

"Field trip to the zoo."

Jill printed, "Zoo Field Trip."

She showed Braden. "Now, what else do we need to do?"

Braden shrugged. "I dunno."

"Well, usually there's a permission slip."

"Oh, yeah." He searched the bottom of his backpack and pulled out a rumpled paper. "Here."

"Why don't we take care of this right now? Remember, 'handle paper only one time and take care of stuff when we're talking about it.' Now, what do you want to ask me to do?"

Braden grinned. "Oh, yeah. Mom, will you sign my permission slip?" He handed the paper to her.

Jill signed it. "Here you go. And where do you need to put it?"

"Uh, let me think." Braden looked at the ceiling. "In my folder." He stuffed it into the front pocket, wrinkling it until it looked like something out of the trash.

Jill decided not to have him straighten the paper. After all, the teacher had a classroom half full of little boys. She understood wrinkled papers.

"That's all I see that you need to do for tomorrow. But we should check your assignment book. It's a good habit to check it even if you think there's nothing on it."

Braden handed the notebook to his mom. "Blank for tomorrow."

"Okay, put everything in your backpack and set it by the door. And you're ready to go outside and play."

Organization Tips

While Jill trains Braden to keep his school stuff organized, to handle papers efficiently, and to keep a calendar, she is also teaching him to prepare for tomorrow, while school is fresh on his mind.

Right now, there are not many items that need to be on his calendar. However, by learning to keep a schedule now, he will be comfortable using one when he's older. By upper elementary, students often have projects, homework, and activities assigned in advance.

Efficiency in handling papers involves two techniques: using an effective filing system and handling papers only once. Right now, the extent of Braden's filing system is the pocket in front of the folder that his teacher sends home each day. His mother will guide him in using a more complex system as he gets older.

I didn't learn the technique of handling papers only once until I was an adult. The idea is, when you open mail, deal with it right then: file it, pay it, or discard it. Jill had Braden get his permission slip signed and returned to his folder the first time he mentioned it. He will have it ready when his teacher asks for it.

As far as organizing his stuff for the next day, Jill told him to put everything into his backpack and park it by the door. In the rush of a school morning, he doesn't need to be hunting the folder he had out on the table the previous afternoon. It's packed and ready to go.

School Readiness Behavior

Four-year-old Michael sat on the colorful rug in the Sunday school classroom. At the back of the room, his mom, Jill, prepared the materials for the craft project that Mrs. Curry, the lead teacher, would use in a minute. Right now, she was reading *Joseph's Coat* to the children. Suddenly Michael stood up and walked away from the group. Mrs. Curry continued to read even though Jill thought she noticed Michael.

Jill looked to see if anyone else was watching. *What will Mrs. Curry think? What is my kid doing? He usually listens when I read a story.* She got up and headed to the table where Michael stood. Leaning down, she whispered, "Michael, what are you doing?"

He whispered his reply. "I was tired of the story."

"You can't just walk away. Go back to the circle. Now."

Michael didn't move.

"Michael."

"Yes ma'am?"

"Go. Now."

Michael folded his arms across his chest. "No." He wasn't whispering now.

Jill turned to see if the other children were looking. They seemed absorbed in the story. She spoke to the other assistant. "The materials are ready, but we'll be back in time for crafts." She took Michael's hand. "Okay, if you're not going back to the group, we'll leave. Come on."

Michael howled. "Don't make me go. I don't want to go."

Jill dragged him to the door, where he put his hands and feet on the frame so she couldn't pull him through. She picked him up and headed down the hall.

By now, Michael guessed he was in trouble. "I'll listen to the story."

"No, you won't."

Jill found an empty room and set him in a chair.

"Mommy, I'll listen to the story."

Jill shook her head. "No. You'll sit right here until it's time for crafts. Then we'll go back. And we'll discuss this when we get home.

For several minutes, Jill and Michael sat in silence. Then Jill asked, "Are you ready to go back to the classroom and do crafts with the other children?

"Yes ma'am."

"You understand that I expect good behavior?"

"Yes ma'am"

Later, when they arrived home, Jill sent Michael to his room. "I'll be there in a few minutes."

Jill went into the kitchen, put on the tea kettle, and sat down at the table. She had a big job ahead of her. She would let Michael stew a little before she talked to him. She realized that though he knew his numbers and colors, he needed some work on soft skills between now and the start of kindergarten.

Sitting Still and Other Soft Skills

Michael starts kindergarten next fall. There will be expectations for his behavior in school. When Jill read to him, she let him leave the couch and play on the floor near her feet. She thought nothing of it until today. He will be expected to stay at his desk or in the reading circle. The teacher won't allow children to wander around the room when she's reading or they're working on assignments.

Michael's behavior when she confronted him also concerned Jill. She could imagine how his teacher would react if he crossed his arms and defiantly told her no.

There are soft skills that children need before starting kindergarten. Although they are not academic skills, they are directly related to academic success.

Soft skills needed before entering kindergarten include:
- Sitting and staying in a chair or at a desk.
- Waiting for the teacher's permission to speak.
- Following the teacher's directions.
- Walking, rather than running, in the classroom and hallways.
- Speaking quietly and courteously.
- Keeping up with supplies, jackets, and other belongings.

Kindergarten teachers tell me they teach many of these skills after a child enters their classrooms. However, the child who already knows how to behave will be ahead of the crowd.

FOUNDATIONS FOR THIS STAGE

- Three school-readiness skills to introduce at this age include organizing things, keeping a calendar, and handling papers.
- "Systems" make organization easier. An example is having dedicated places to store things.
- At this age, after school is the best time to organize what must be done for the next day.
- Begin calendaring activities early by letting your child

tell you what and where to write. Include family activities such as "Camping Trip" or "Grandma's Visit."

- Readiness for kindergarten includes certain soft skills, which can be practiced at home.
- Empower your child to do every part of these tasks that he is able to do on his own.

FAQs

I try to get my four-year-old son to sit by me on the couch when I read. He complains and begs to get down on the floor. The conflict turns our story time into a hassle. How can I do this?

Getting your son to sit beside you for short periods of time may be a hassle, but it's better to address the issue before he starts to school.

Begin by explaining: "Next year when you are a big boy and go to kindergarten, there will be times you have to stay in your seat. We are going to practice that now so you'll be ready for school." Treat the training like a game.

Use a timer. Begin by having him sit beside you for three minutes. After the timer goes off, he can push his cars around on the floor—or another quiet activity—while you read. Each week add a minute to his sitting time. You can let him chart his progress on a graph. By the time he begins kindergarten, he should be able to stay in his seat, focused on one task for fifteen minutes. Remember that he does not have to be *perfectly* still, but he should not be standing on his head or hanging off the couch.

I would love to help my children get organized. Their backpacks are messy. They forget to bring home im-

portant papers and books. How can they be prepared for school if they can't organize their school stuff? The problem is, I'm not organized either, so teaching what I don't know is hard.

You can learn together. Some of the most organized people I know were not born that way, but they worked at learning the necessary skills.

Scholastic has an excellent article on teaching organization,[35]

Begin by creating a family calendar posted in a central location. Next, get individual calendars for yourself and for each of your children. For them, consider spiral assignment books. They are inexpensive and well-suited to kids. Summer stuff can go on the family calendar.

Try to devote a few minutes at the end of each week, updating your calendars for the coming week. Help your children do theirs. Additional commitments can be added throughout the week.

Invest in some folders to organize papers. Spend a few weeks getting accustomed to using folders for all the paper that comes into your life. For children, use file folders closed on the sides so contents don't fall out. Walk your children through the process.

As you go through each of the steps with your children, you learn together. Being disorganized yourself can be an advantage because you understand his lack of organization.

A note about electronic calendars: I love mine, but there is something wonderful about one I can write on. Paper calendars or assignment books are more effective for teaching children. When they're older and competent using paper versions, they can switch if they desire.

The good news is that at this age your children will think organizing for school is fun. Teaching them preparedness at six is easier than at sixteen.

PARENT GOALS FOR THIS STAGE

- Practice the "handle papers once" rule with your own papers and mail.
- Shop with your child for a calendar, one that is small, colorful, and easy to use.
- Establish a system, color-coded if possible, for organizing papers and supplies.
- Teach your child the soft skills needed in kindergarten. Check with your local school for additional skills needed.

ACTION TO EMPOWER

I will empower my child by . . .
(allow your children to choose the organizational skill they want to learn first).

_____

_____

_____

_____

_____

_____

Create an Island of Calm in Each Day

What is this life so full of care,
We don't have time to stand and stare.
W.H. Davies

Goals for Age Eighteen:

- Acknowledges need in personal life for some down-time.
- Knows how to include unstructured time.
- Manages a task "in the moment" without stress.
- Doesn't feel guilty when relaxing.

Deep Couch and Deep Questions

"Mommy, why was Anna's mama crying?" Five-year-old Emma scrunched closer to her mom, Rebecca, while three-year-old Ben drove a model car along the edge of the sofa cushion.

118

"Honey, she was talking to me about Anna's grandmother. Remember, I told you she's very sick. She's not only Anna's grandmother. She's also Mrs. Patterson's mother.

Ben stopped his play and looked up at his mom. He climbed onto the sofa beside her. Rebecca put her arms around Emma and Ben as they snuggled into the depths of the couch. She kissed the brown curls on the top of each head. "I love you guys."

Emma leaned away to look at her mom. "Is Anna's grandmother going to die?"

"Yes, she could die. She is old and sick—a kind of sickness that means her body is wearing out. But Anna's grandmother is a Christian and looks forward to going to Heaven."

Ben looked up at his mom. "Is Grammie going to die?"

"You know, kids, we never know when someone will die. But Grammie is healthy and will probably live a long time. She says she plans to dance at your weddings."

Rebecca pulled her children close. "Why don't we pray for Anna's grandmother right now? The children cuddled deeper into their mom's embrace as Rebecca began. "Lord, thank you for Anna's grandmother's life. Today, she is really sick, and we ask you to be with her. If it's time for her to go to Heaven, we thank you that she knows you. If she has more time on Earth, we thank you for helping her get well. We especially thank you for taking care of her. Comfort her family and guide her doctors. In Jesus' name, amen.

Emma wiggled out of her mom's embrace. "At school today, Hannah told me she's going to have a baby sister. I want a baby sister too."

Rebecca sighed. "Emma, you had a baby brother. Then he grew up into a big boy. Hannah's baby sister will grow up too."

Ben sat up and puffed out his chest. "I'm a big boy, Mommy."

"Yes you are, Ben."

Rebecca and her children talked about school for a few more

119

minutes. When she sensed that they had covered all the topics they needed to discuss, she took her arms from around them and got up. "Let's go check your backpacks to see if you have reading to do."

After-School Downtime

Rebecca uses the first few minutes after the kids get home from school to let them download their day. They grab a snack and head to the couch to wait for their mom. She doesn't set a time or rush them through their "snuggle time." When there's silence, she allows it to linger, avoiding the urge to fill the space with talk. She listens to them and follows where their conversation leads.

One lesson that Rebecca is teaching her children is the importance of including some unstructured time in their lives. Too many people live with every second scheduled. Rebecca and her husband do not want that for their children.

Activity Overload

"Kick it. Kick it now, Taylor." Melissa jumped out of her folding chair. She and her friend Stephanie were watching their girls play soccer. The score was unofficial, because someone had decided there should be no losers. However, everyone knew how many points each team scored. Right now, Taylor and Kayla's team was two goals behind. Taylor kicked the ball out of bounds, and Melissa sat down.

Stephanie was scrolling through her phone. "I've got two messages from friends wanting to know if I plan to let Kayla take ballet. I don't know, Melissa. It seems like we're rushing all the time with what we already have. The ballet sign-up is next week. What are you going to do?"

"We haven't decided, but Taylor has already asked about it. Her dad told her he thought she had enough, and I think I agree. At least we still have a few days to decide."

A whistle signaled the end of the game. Both women looked up as the team rushed off the field. Coach called the girls around and talked quietly in a huddle as two parents got out end-of-game snacks.

Taylor had a juice box in one hand and a bag of Goldfish in the other as she ran to where Melissa and Stephanie waited. "Mom, Sarah and Alexis are going to take ballet. I want to too."

"We'll talk with Dad about it tonight."

"Please, please." Taylor looked at Stephanie. "Kayla wants to do ballet too, Mrs. Howell. We could go together."

Melissa and Stephanie looked at each other, their own frustration mirrored in each other's eyes.

Melissa wondered, *How do I balance the need for downtime with the desire to do it all?*

Stephanie spoke first. "Like your mom said, Taylor, this is something we need to discuss with your dads. We have another week before sign-up."

That evening after the children were in bed, Melissa and her husband, Jeremy, sat down. They had to decide if they should allow Taylor to enroll in another after-school activity.

"I don't know, Jeremy. When you have to work late, I'm not sure I can handle something else. With the boys and Taylor, that's three afternoons plus Saturday games. I know you help when you get home in time, but there are those other days."

Jeremy leaned forward with his elbows on his knees. "What if we miss the one thing that ignites her passion? She might have the body or whatever it takes to be great in ballet, and we never let her get involved. I guess that's my concern."

Melissa leaned against the back of the couch. "I know. I worry about that too. But I also don't want our kids so busy that they never have downtime in their lives. That's where creativity thrives and more importantly, where they hear from God. I don't think he wants to shout over the ruckus."

"Yeah, I know. Sometimes I'm too busy to hear God. I don't want to pass that on to our kids."

"I have an idea. She's in soccer now and plans to play T-ball in the spring. How about if we let her choose between ballet and T-ball next semester? At this age, we can limit her to one activity per semester, but let her change each season. What do you think?"

The Tough Balancing Act

Melissa and Jeremy are fighting the pressure to do and be all. And Taylor is only in first grade.

True, if a child is going to excel in something, it's good to start early. Wasn't Tiger Woods swinging a golf club when he was two years old? However, as far as I know, Tiger was not enrolled in violin lessons and gymnastics while he learned to play golf. He expressed interest and was encouraged by his dad in only one pursuit—golf.

Melissa and Jeremy are wise to be concerned about overloading their six-year-old daughter as well as the entire family. They did the right thing by making the decision together, away from other parents and Taylor. They will present a united front when they talk to their daughter.

FOUNDATIONS FOR THIS STAGE

- Children need unstructured time every day, and some of that time should include physical closeness with a parent.
- Choosing a regular place to "chill" gives kids a way of signaling to parents their need to talk or just be together.
- At this age, children do well with only one structured extracurricular activity.
- Decisions about children's involvement should be made away from pressure from the kids and other parents. Only after a decision is made should it be communicated to the child.
- It's a good idea to let kids switch to a new activity each semester unless they are passionate about the current activity.

FAQs

I would love to have only one after-school activity for each of my three kids. If I'm lucky, I'm able to schedule two kids on the same day, but even then, I still use up two days' of after-school time. But the pressure is on, even at this early age, to be in so many activities. My friends are preparing their kids for the competitive world of league sports and college applications. I feel I must jump into the competition. What can I do?

Only you can make these decisions for your family. Here are some suggestions that might help you prioritize:

- Whether you teach your children to pack everything possible into each twenty-four-hour day or teach them to spend some daily downtime, know that you are setting the habit for their lifetimes. It will be hard to break that habit when they are seniors in high school or young professionals.
- In regard to how you structure your family's life, you may choose to be radically different from your peers. In doing so, you teach your children an important lesson: dare to be different when you know what is right for you.
- Rather than initiate activities you believe your children would find interesting, listen to and observe them to see where their interests lie. Sometimes in our enthusiasm, we jump ahead, denying them the joy of finding their own interests.
- The happiest adults are those who find their passion and give it their all, rather than scattering themselves over many half-done endeavors. Teach your children to focus on fewer pursuits that engage their greatest passion, and you will give them a tremendous gift that will last a lifetime.

I like the idea of snuggle time, but we're too busy. When we first get home, I need to start dinner, see what the kids have to do for the next day, and go through the mail. Since I work, I have things to do after dinner. Suddenly, it's time for the kids to get ready for bed.

I know schedules are packed. The point of this chapter is twofold:
- To recognize the importance of teaching children about unstructured time. At this age, they are forming habits for a lifetime.

- To figure out how to include unstructured time in overloaded schedules.

I believe there is only one way to unpack a family schedule—by prayerfully considering each item in the schedule to determine what can be cut or reduced. Don't forget to include regular activities that might not appear on a calendar—such as chores, reading, and outdoor time. Go after that overloaded schedule in the same way that you unmercifully rid a closet of unused "stuff."

If you do this for your family, you will find that blessings abound as you settle into a calmer, more rewarding family schedule.

PARENT GOALS FOR THIS STAGE

- Eliminate some commitments from your own schedule.
- Find a spot in each day for unstructured time with your kids.
- Set expectations with kids in advance so they do not go into a season expecting to do it all.

ACTION TO EMPOWER

I will empower my child by . . .
(give an example of how you will let your child help make decisions about activities).

_____

_____

_____

_____

Section 6: Relationships

Having someone wonder where you are
when you don't come home at night is a very old human need.
Margaret Mead

God created us to be in relationships—with him and with people. We cannot thrive—or sometimes even survive—without relationships. The first relationships that children experience are with parents and siblings. After parents and extended family, they venture into the world of peers. What they learn in these childhood friendships forms the foundation for all future relationships.

Between Two Generations

*Beneath its myriad rules, the fundamental purpose of etiquette
is to make the world a pleasanter place to live in,
and you a more pleasant person to live with.*
Emily Post

Goals for Age Eighteen

- Understands that the foundation of good manners is making others feel valued.
- Accepts that adults have privileges that children and teens do not.
- Shows respect to all, especially those who are elevated in the hierarchy of privilege.

Little Ways to Respect Adults

Four-year-old Addison ran into the kitchen, where her mom, Rachel, was preparing dinner. "Mommy, may I go into your room and leave Daddy a surprise on the bed?" She held up the painting

127

she'd made of her dad standing at the backyard grill.

"That's nice, Addison. Let me see if it's dry." Rachel laid her knife on the cutting board and felt the painting. "I don't want wet paint on the comforter, but I think it's fine. Here you go. Just be sure you close the bedroom door when you leave."

Addison skipped down the hall toward her parents' bedroom. As she went, she hummed a song she'd learned in preschool.

Rachel smiled. It was good to hear Addison happy again.

Just recently, Jeff's mother had been hospitalized with an infection around her heart. For several days, the entire family was on edge. One night Rachel walked into Addison's room and found her crying.

"Addie, what's wrong?"

"I don't want Gran to be sick."

Rachel sat on the bed and gathered Addison into her arms. "None of us want her to be sick, sweetheart. That's why we've been praying for her and her doctors."

"I heard Daddy talking on the phone to Aunt Kate. I don't like Daddy to be sad."

Rachel wiped a tear off Addison's cheek. "Daddy's always so strong, I know it's hard for you to hear him worrying about his mom."

"He called her *Mother* instead of Gran."

"I think he only says "Gran" when he's talking to you. I call her Gladys, Daddy calls her Mother, and you call her Gran."

Addison giggled. "Gran has lots of names. Grampa calls her Possum."

Rachel chuckled. "Yes, he does." She helped Addison get under the covers. "Now, it's time to go to sleep. I'm going to pray for Gran. What else do you want me to pray about?" Before turning out the lamp and going back downstairs, Rachel prayed with Addison.

Remembering that incident reminded Rachel that children

sometimes overhear adult conversations and keep their worries inside. During the time that Gladys was recovering, Rachel made a point to talk to Addison about Gran each evening before she prayed with her.

Rachel looked up from chopping veggies when she heard Addison coming back down the hallway.

"Mommy, I put the painting on the bed. It's a surprise. Don't tell Daddy."

"I won't. And I bet he'll love the picture. Maybe he'll grill for us again this weekend—just because he likes the picture so much."

Teach that Adulthood is to Be Respected

In the context of daily living, and especially during Addison's worry about her grandmother, Rachel teaches important lessons about respect for parents and other adults.

Rachel and Jeff keep their bedroom as a place only for themselves. One way to do that is to make the sofa the place to cuddle. The children are taught not to go into the parents' bedroom without permission. They are not allowed to take friends into the room. The result of this respect for the parents' room is an awareness that there are adult privileges and there are child privileges. Adult privileges are better and something to look forward to in their own adulthood.

The use of special names to show respect include the names for adult family members and close friends. Rachel and Jeff do not allow their children to call them or other adults by first names. The exception is that a close family friend might be called Aunt or Uncle with a first name. Other adults are called Mr. or Mrs. with their last name. When teens are in positions of authority over them they use Miss or Mr. with a first name. They call their babysitter Miss Jessica.

Rachel and Jeff call adults by their special names when speaking to their children. They do this to teach them the name they should use. A mother who calls her mother-in-law by her first name will find her children doing the same instead of using a "grandmother name."

All these guidelines about names are another way of teaching children that adults have gained a place of honor by becoming adults. When children learn these lessons at home, they are more likely to respect teachers and other adults in positions of authority

Caleb Practices Being a Gentleman

Caleb ran past an elderly couple to get to the restaurant door. He pulled the door open and gave them a big smile.

"Well thank you, young fella." The man stepped back to let his wife go through the door first. "How old are you, young man?"

"I'm six." Caleb stood straighter and puffed out his chest.

"You're certainly a fine gentleman for a six-year-old."

Caleb continued to hold the door while two teen girls went through. They were busy texting and said nothing to Caleb. He waited as his mother, grandmother, and older sister approached the restaurant. Each one thanked him as she walked through the door.

Caleb followed his family to a table and pulled out a chair for his grandmother.

"Thank you, Caleb."

Caleb looked to see that his mother and sister were already seated and then sat in his own chair. He was happy to hold a chair for his mother, but he had let it be known in the past that he didn't think he should have to do that for his sister.

"Mom, those girls didn't say anything when I held the door for them."

"I saw that, Caleb. They were busy texting and didn't see you."

"It made me not want to keep holding the door."

"I know, but we try to do what's right even when others don't."

Zoe looked at her little brother. "Also, I bet if they had looked up and seen you, they would have thanked you." She glanced at her mother and laughed. "And now is the time for Mom to say, 'That's just one more reason we shouldn't mess with our phones in public places.' Right, Mom?"

Mom looked at Grandmother. "She's got me figured out, huh?"

The four of them enjoyed lunch with frequent laughter punctuating their conversation. When they finished, the waitress asked if they needed anything else and left their ticket.

Grandmother opened her purse. "This is my treat, but I hate standing in line to pay. Will you do that for me, Caleb?"

"Yes ma'am."

Grandmother handed the ticket and money to Caleb. "You can wait for change, because you should get a little over five dollars."

With a smile spread from ear to ear, Caleb headed toward the cashier to pay for the meal.

"You're doing a great job with these kids, Jennifer. Caleb is learning some manners that are important. And Zoe is learning to be gracious. There's a fine line between doing what's correct by the books and doing what makes someone else feel good." She looked at her granddaughter. "You sat down before Caleb got to you, which kept him from having to hold your chair. That's not only thoughtful, but also gracious. And I am sure he appreciated it.

Lessons in Showing Respect Begin Early

Good manners have one purpose—to make someone else feel valued. Whether it's not talking with a mouth full of food or holding a door, every example of manners is about our relationships

131

with other people.

There is a hierarchy in manners, with age trumping youth and female trumping male. Caleb is young and male. Therefore, when he goes out to lunch with three females, he has ample opportunities to practice his manners.

In today's politically correct climate, some women do not want men to defer to them, but most feel honored when men hold doors, pull out chairs, or step back to let them walk in front. We can teach our boys the guidelines and hope they meet girls who like good manners.

Children learn their manners most easily when they begin practicing in the preschool years. When children arrive at school with good manners, teachers notice. If the habit is well-established by middle school, teachers are impressed. I find that most kids need to score all the points they can at that age. Good manners are a big help toward that goal.

Other important rules that are not addressed in the story above include not interrupting when someone is talking, using quiet voices in certain places, and acknowledging a guest coming into one's presence by making eye contact and speaking. In many cases, it is appropriate to stand for a guest.

FOUNDATIONS FOR THIS STAGE

- Children and adults are on different levels in the family hierarchy. It is not only okay for adults to have extra privileges, but it is good for children to be aware that adulthood has its perks.
- The parents' bedroom should be set apart as a place that is exclusively for them.
- The first manners taught to young children are saying please and thank you. And even when they can only dic-

tate and draw a scribble, children need to write thank-you notes.

- Children should address adults with respect. That includes calling them Mr. or Mrs. unless they are close enough to be called a family name. They also should answer an adult with "Yes ma'am" and "No sir."
- Parents teach children to use family names by using those names in the presence of the children.

FAQs

I think it sounds great to teach children manners. I am all for this, but I don't see anyone else practicing them with their children. Won't my children stick out around their peers?

Yes, they will. The good news is, they will stick out in a positive way. If their friends tease them, they may have the wrong friends. Adults will be favorably impressed. Good manners cover a multitude of goof-ups.

For example, if your child has to ask a special favor such as making up a test at a different time, the teacher will be favorably disposed to him if he is well-mannered. This may not be right or fair, but it is a fact.

Years ago, I had a middle-school student who was having trouble with several teachers. One teacher in particular seemed to have it in for him. The student and I came up with a plan. He would go out of his way to display gracious manners to the teacher for two weeks and see what happened. We planned and plotted what it meant to use good manners.

At the end of the first week, I met with him to see how things were going. He said, "I think Mr. Johnston is nicer than he used to be." At the end of the second week, the student said, "Something good must have happened to Mr. Johnston to make him happier. He's been nice to me all week."

The young man assured me that he had changed nothing with the teacher except his manners. That included a cheerful greeting each day as he entered the classroom. Good manners do matter.

I'd love to have a well-mannered kid, but I think he wouldn't fit in with our family. We have a lot to learn to have good manners. I looked at a well-known author's book on manners and was overwhelmed. I need a simple starting place. Can you give me a suggestion?

Susan Merrill has a website called imom.com. One of the great features of her website is printable pages. For example, she has a page of social manners[36] for young children. It's catchy and colorful and can be printed to post where kids can see it. I love this list because it is simple yet comprehensive for small children.

Carol McD. Wallace's book on manners[37] is easy reading and hits the nail on the head as to what is important and what can be overlooked in some situations. She approaches the subject with humor and personal stories.

The Emily Post Institute publishes a book of manners for children.[38] Although it is a more extensive treatment of manners, it still teaches etiquette on the same premise as their foremother: the purpose of manners is "to make the world a pleasanter place . . . and you a more pleasant person."[39]

The Internet, the Web, and the public library are great resources for parents' how-to books about manners as well as books written for the kids. At this age, children are open to learning about manners from a book. Not so much by middle school.

Remember that manners are all about making someone else feel valued. And that is the foundation of good relationships. You can learn manners together as a fun family project. Perhaps you can have one "manners meal" a week, during which you practice what you have already learned and also learn an additional way to make others feel special.

PARENT GOALS FOR THIS STAGE

- Decide what manners you will teach first.
- Be sure you understand the purpose of manners.
- Plan ways to practice manners before requiring them in public.
- Relax and enjoy the process. If your children mess up, remind them that they are learning and can try again next time.
- Build incentives, such as praise and celebration, into the process.

ACTION TO EMPOWER

I will empower my child by . . .
(give one example in which you will let your child demonstrate good manners and respect to someone).

_____

_____

_____

_____

_____

_____

Friendships with Peers

Things are never quite as scary when you have a best friend.
Calvin in *Calvin and Hobbes* by Bill Watterson

Goals for Age Eighteen

- Adapts to different sets of rules depending on where he is.
- Knows how to be a good host and a good guest.
- Feels comfortable in both leader and follower roles.

Red Corvette or Blue Camaro

"Here's a car for you." Four-year-old Luke held out a blue Camaro Hot Wheels.

His friend Josh took the car and sat by the track.

Luke rummaged through a box, then walked into the kitchen where both moms were sitting at the table. "Mom, where's my red Corvette?"

Diane raised her eyebrows and turned to her son. "I believe I

136

found it in a pocket, Luke. It's still in the laundry room."

"Thanks." Luke headed down the hall.

Josh's mom, Michelle, laughed. "I told my family I was going keep everything I find in pockets. Then, I'll sell it back to the owner. I haven't done it yet, but I thought it sounded like a good idea."

Luke returned to the playroom with his car. "Let's have a race. You pick the side you want."

Josh scooted around to sit by one side of the track. "Can I have that car?"

"No, the Corvette's my favorite."

"I want the red one."

"My dad says Camaros are cool."

"But, I want the red one." Standing up, Josh dropped the Camaro and raised his voice. "Mommy, Luke won't share."

Michelle headed to the playroom. Diane was close behind. By the time they got there, the two boys were in a standoff. Both mothers sat on the floor to help the boys reach a compromise.

With encouragement, the boys decided to take turns using the Corvette. They were soon back at play.

Play Dates

Luke and Josh have a play date once a week. Sometimes, the mothers take time for coffee while the kids play, but more often, one mother gets to run errands, treat herself to a manicure, or meet her husband for lunch.

Play dates are important for children's social training. They learn to share, take turns, and do projects together with parental guidance.

Both boys have siblings to play with, but there's a difference. In a family, the younger child tends to be a follower while the older one is the leader. Play dates with peers give kids opportunities to relate to someone in different ways than they do at home.

Before parents set up play dates, they need to address some questions:

- Are there food allergies or medications that need to be considered?
- Do the children understand that they will follow the house rules and obey the host parent?
- Are all emergency contact and medical information available to the host parent?
- Will there be equitable division of who is host? If not, is there a way to compensate for the difference?
- Is there an understanding about who pays for expenses, the host or the guest, if the host takes the children to something that costs money (movie, pool, ice cream)?
- Are both families in agreement about child-rearing practices such as use of electronics, exposure to media, and other worldview issues?

As they get older, Luke and Josh will play together with less supervision. But at this age, the host parent needs to be a room away and ready to intervene and guide them as they learn social skills.

I Want Some Chips

"Mom, it's hot outside. May we have something to drink?" Six-year-old Jake and his friends, Noah and Daniel, burst into the kitchen. Their faces were red, their shirts drenched, and their odor pungent.

"You guys look like you need to cool off a few minutes. Why don't you sit at the table? Jake, get the Gatorade, and I'll get some glasses. I'll cut up apples too."

Jake brought a big bottle of orange Gatorade to the table and

138

filled glasses. The boys grabbed them and began chugging.

Daniel pulled his shirt up and wiped his face. "Mrs. Hudgins, do you have some chips?"

Laura set down the bowl of apple slices. "I may have some chips stuck away somewhere, but I'd rather feed you apples with your Gatorade. I'll give you a spoonful of peanut butter (good to know food allergies of each child) to go with your apples, if you'd like."

Noah looked up. "I've never had peanut butter in a spoon. Is it good?"

Jake ran to the cabinet to get spoons. "It's even better than on bread. Try it."

Daniel folded his arms across his chest. "I want chips. I don't like peanut butter."

"Well, Daniel, this is the snack we're having today: Gatorade, apples, and PB. Your choice. Any of those three things, but no chips."

"My mom lets me have chips all the time."

"Daniel, do you remember when we started letting you guys play at one another's houses and we talked about house rules?"

"Yes ma'am."

"What your moms and I decided is that you would learn to accept the rules of the home where you're playing. Those rules may be different in different homes, but you need to follow them—even when they're not exactly like your own. I know that's tough—like when you'd rather have chips for snacks."

Laura reached for the spoons and the jar of peanut butter. "How about trying apples and peanut butter today?"

Daniel sighed. "Oh, okay. I'll try."

139

House Rules or My Rules?

Laura is hosting the play date for Jake and his two friends. The other mothers have a few hours to do as they wish. It's more than getting a break two weeks out of three. The boys are learning to play together. They are also learning other lessons:

House rules: The mothers trust one another to teach moral behavior, but they do not expect each home to have exactly the same rules. This exposes the boys to environments that are slightly different from their own. They learn that in one home they may take food into the family room, but at another they must eat at the table. They eat junk food at one home and healthy food at another. They even shed their shoes at the door and play in sock feet at one of the houses.

Playing with a group of three: Although not addressed in the story above, there are unique challenges when three children play together. Two tend to unite against one. Each mother is aware of this tendency and will spend time helping the boys have inclusive play that does not leave out one.

Being the host child: Certain responsibilities fall to the child who is the host. For example, Jake asked for drinks on behalf of his friends and poured the Gatorade. Playing host is an important skill.

Being the guest child: There are unique skills to be learned about being a guest. In the story above, Daniel was struggling in the guest role.

FOUNDATIONS FOR THIS STAGE

- Children at this age need regular play dates with peers, even if they have siblings for playmates.
- Play dates give children the opportunity to try on the

roles of leader and follower, guest and host.

- Parents need to establish ground rules and share important information. If the rules are set up in advance of the first play date, there will be less friction.
- Children need to know the play-date rules that apply to them, such as minding the host parent. Communicate the rules to all the children in front of all the parents.
- It is important to ensure that the mothers do equal sharing of the host responsibility. Although it's best for each mother to do her share, sometimes that's impossible. In that case, there should a way to equalize the inequity, even if it means that one pays the other.

FAQs

I set up play dates with a friend who also has a three-year-old daughter, but she takes advantage of me. I keep her child much more than she keeps mine. I also suspect that she doesn't spend much time supervising and teaching our daughters when they are playing.

Your question is an example of why it's so important to set the ground rules in advance. But believe me, most everyone goes into play-date arrangements casually. Then they find themselves in a situation they don't know how to handle with grace.

I suggest you invite her to stay for coffee one day so you can talk about your daughters and their play dates. Frame it as a time to evaluate how things are going. When you have the girls settled into their play, say something like, "Kelly, we've been having play dates for our girls for three months now. I thought it would be good to talk about how it's going, what they're learning, and how we can improve the arrangement."

141

Allow her to talk first. Listen to what she has to say. Finally, say, "I want to apologize that we didn't discuss this topic in advance, but there are some things that I feel aren't going right. It may just be my perception, and that's why I want to hear your ideas too.

"For one thing, I would feel better if we worked out a schedule so we knew in advance when each of us was hosting a play date. We need to share equally how many times we keep the girls. When we first started, you had some special situations when you needed me to keep Madison more than you kept Hailey. But I'm getting behind on the things I need to do. I would like for us to go back to alternating every week. Is that okay with you?

"Also, I would like for us to spend a few minutes together when we pick up our daughters, sharing what our girls did, the conflicts they had, and how they were resolved. I know there are times that I have had to do 'conflict resolution,' and it would be helpful for each of us to know what the other is doing. Would that work for you?"

Later, if she says something has come up and she can't keep the girls, graciously offer to postpone the play date until the next date when she can keep them.

This may seem harsh, but the purpose of play dates is not being met if only one parent hosts. Of course, you may discover that you are the only parent willing to invite other children to your home. In that case, you must decide if you want to do that. Being the home where all the children hang out has some distinct advantages, especially when they're teens. It may be that you want to be that parent.

We once had a play date arrangement with a pre-school friend of my son's, but we had to stop. Each time my son came home, he was disrespectful in the way he talked to me and his dad. I realized that he was picking

142

up those habits from his friend, whose mother let her son speak disrespectfully to her.

You have three choices:

- Stop the play-date arrangement.
- Talk to the mother. This may not be effective. If she's allowing her son to speak disrespectfully to her, the chances that your words will change her parenting methods are slim. But you may want to try.
- Talk to your son and let him know that if his friend behaves badly, he is still responsible for following your rules. Rather than copy his friend's behavior, he must continue to speak with respect to his own parents and to the host parent. Nor should you allow his friend to speak disrespectfully to you.

At this age, I recommend the first choice. By the time your son is about ten years old, you will need to teach him that he has rules to follow that are often different from the rules others follow. That is an important lesson to learn before reaching middle school, but for a preschooler, it's a bit difficult.

PARENT GOALS FOR THIS STAGE

- Find friends who have children the age of your children and a worldview like yours.
- Invite your friend or friends to get together to discuss play dates.
- Establish guidelines. This can be done somewhat informally, but be sure that all issues are covered.
- Talk to your own child about the responsibilities of a host and a guest.

143

- Discuss with your child house rules and how they may be different in each home.

ACTION TO EMPOWER

I will empower my child by . . .
(give an example of how you will let your child make decisions about play dates such as special activities or planning a snack).

_____

_____

_____

_____

_____

_____

From Different Planets, but Not So Fast

In the United States today, there is a pervasive tendency to treat children as adults, and adults as children. The options of children are thus steadily expanded, while those of adults are progressively constricted. The result is unruly children and childish adults.
Thomas Szasz

Goals for Age Eighteen

- Embraces equality of both sexes.
- Understands and appreciates the difference between men and women.
- Is able to have friends of the opposite sex without romantic involvement.
- Relates openly and authentically in a romantic relationship.

Guy's Jobs versus Girl's Jobs

Megan walked to the door of the family room and stopped. Five-year-old Matthew and his friend Eva were leaning over his Lego table, building a town. As Megan listened to their conversation, she realized that they were unaware of her presence.

"Eva," Matthew said, "you can't help build the houses. That's a guy's job. You can watch."

Eva stood tall with her hands on her hips. "Girls can too build." She began adding blocks to the house that Matthew was working on.

"No. You pick out the colors for the next house I build."

Eva calmly picked up more blocks to add to the construction.

Matthew pushed her hands away.

Eva pushed back.

Megan decided it was time to intervene. "Hey, guys. What are you building?"

Eva presented her complaint. "Mrs. Baker, Matthew won't let me build houses. He says that's a guy's job."

Without saying anything, Matthew continued to add bricks to his project.

Megan waited a moment. "Matthew?"

Eva waited, looking first at Megan and then at Matthew.

Megan cleared her throat. "Matthew. I'm speaking to you. Please acknowledge that you hear me."

"Yes ma'am."

"When we have friends over to play, it's important to share toys. Eva wants to help you build the houses."

"She's just a girl. She's supposed to do girl things."

Megan sat on the floor. "Both of you come here and sit by me. Let's talk about this. Girls and boys can both be anything they want to be. There may be more builders who are men, but that doesn't mean that a girl can't build houses. And there are boys who grow up to be decorators.

Megan raised her hand. "What's that?"

"A decorator? That's what Matthew wants you to be—a decorator. That's someone who chooses colors, furniture, and fabrics to make a home look pretty. They are using artistic ability to decide what looks good."

Matthew looked at his mom. "Could I be one of those—a decorator?"

"You could, Matthew."

Megan touched her temple with a forefinger. "I have an idea. How about if you pretend the two of you own a company that builds houses. You can work together to decide on colors and style. That means you decide if it's two-story, how many doors, and where the chimney is. Once you decide that, you can build together. Take turns being the boss for each house. And remember, even when you are not the boss, you still do part of the work. She looked at Eva. "Do you think that will work?"

"Yes ma'am."

Turning toward her son, she asked, "How about you, Matthew?"

Matthew nodded. "Okay. Eva, do you want to be the first boss?"

Megan stood to leave as the children set to work on their first joint venture in homebuilding. As Megan went back to the other room, she pondered where her son had come up with the idea that men and women had career limitations based on gender. *I must redouble my efforts to expose Matthew and his siblings to a variety of careers.*

Surely in the twenty-first century, our children can learn that the sky's the limit for both boys and girls.

Gender Equality in the Twenty-First Century

Matthew caught Megan off-guard by his attitude toward gender equality in careers. His dad taught school, and she was an attorney working from home. Those seemed like jobs that broke the gender stereotype, yet somehow Matthew decided Eva should not be allowed to build houses.

Observing children, we see that more boys choose trucks as toys while more girls choose dolls. Boys generally choose rougher play than girls. But there are exceptions. And there should not be arbitrary rules that assign children to choices based on their sex.

It's important to encourage children when they choose non-traditional interests. Sometimes parents have predetermined goals, but the children have other ideas. It's wise to help children explore their stated interests, as well as some they might not have considered.

Subtle influences affect how our children form many of their beliefs. Matthew may have formed his understanding of gender roles from a grandparent, a friend's parents, or even media. His parents' silence on their own non-traditional careers may have influenced him.

Perhaps in another generation, we will have wiped out that kind of stereotyping, but for now we need to be conscious of what our children learn.

Olivia's Boyfriend

Olivia spotted her grandmother as soon as she stepped through the revolving doors. Olivia's mother, Jami, and Olivia were meeting Grana at the airport. Even though they kept up with one another by Skype, they only got together once or twice a year. Six-year-old Olivia was so excited, she had trouble sleeping the past two nights.

Mom waited for Grana's luggage while Grana listened to Olivia's plans for her visit. Olivia was talking a mile a minute about all she had planned, making Grana think she might have to stay all summer.

An hour later, they were at home and unloading the car when six-year-old Jake from next door showed up. Never shy, Jake approached Grana and asked, "What should I call you?"

"Well, I guess you can call me Grana or Mrs. Lewis."

Olivia looked at Jake as if he had stepped off Mars. "You can't call her Grana. She's my Grana."

Jake nodded. "Okay."

"What's your name, young man?"

"Jake."

Olivia smiled at Jake before she spoke to her grandmother. "We're in the same class."

"I see."

Jake's mother called him home, and the family went inside.

Olivia was dancing up and down. "I made a surprise for you, Grana. I painted a picture, and it's on your bed."

Grana headed to the guest room just as Mom called from the kitchen. "Olivia, come help me set the table while Grana gets settled in."

Grana came into the kitchen about the same time Dad arrived home. "How's my favorite son-in-law?"

"Great. How about you, Joan?"

"Surprisingly well, thank you. I thought I'd be tired after four hours in airports and planes. I'll sleep well tonight, I'm sure."

Grana smiled at Olivia and looked back at Dad. "I see your daughter has a little boyfriend."

"Uh, what?"

"The little boy next door. They're so cute together."

Olivia looked surprised. "He's not a boyfriend. He's just Jake."

Grana chuckled. "That's what they always say: 'We're just friends.' You shouldn't be embarrassed. He's a cute boyfriend."

Dad looked uncomfortable. "Uh, Joan, so how was your trip? Any late planes or annoying seat mates?"

"Oh, everything went well. It was just long."

Grana looked at Olivia. "So did Jake give you a valentine or do anything else boyfriends do for their girlfriends?"

"We have a rule. If you give valentines to anyone, you have to give to the whole class."

Mom stepped away from her dinner prep. "Uh, Mom. Can you come with me just a moment? I have something to tell you in private."

As she left the room, she looked at Olivia. "Sweetheart, can you finish setting the table for me? We're nearly ready to eat."

Jami and her mom walked into the guest room and closed the door. Jami gently explained to her mom that she and Olivia's dad thought Olivia was too young to be encouraged to have a boyfriend. They wanted her to have lots of friends who happened to be both boys and girls. Joan was surprised, but said she would respect their wishes and not mention it again. They were laughing together when they returned to the kitchen.

Just Friends

In the past, talk of boyfriend-girlfriend pairings began almost as early as children learned to walk. Now, parents realize that it's unhealthy to push children into adult-style opposite-sex relationships.

When these children are adults, they will be with people of both sexes in the workplace and the community. They need to learn to relate to friends and co-workers as equals, without bringing romance into the mix.

Olivia's parents want her to have healthy friends-only relationships with the boys in her neighborhood and at school. Then when she is old enough to look at boys as possible mates, she will have seen many different personalities. She will be less eager to grab the first guy who tells her she's pretty.

FOUNDATIONS FOR THIS STAGE

- Play dates at this age should include the opposite sex part of the time.
- All types of play can be enjoyed by both sexes.
- Household chores should be assigned without considering gender.
- Young children should not be encouraged to have a boyfriend-girlfriend relationship.
- Parents are in charge of how their children are raised. If necessary, they may have to explain their child-rearing philosophy to grandparents and other relatives.

FAQs

I live in a town where fifth graders—and their parents—make a big deal about homecoming. I have seen ten-year-old girls wearing mums nearly as big as they are and sitting with a boy when both would rather be with their friends. I have about four years to build a case for avoiding this fiasco with my own child. Any ideas to help me do that?

Begin by talking to the parents of your child's friends—both boys and girls—now. Remind them that children in elementary and middle school should be exploring sports and the arts, learning which school subjects interest them, and having fun. You said you have four years to build your case. One point to include is that kids who have interests such as sports, band, or theater are less likely to get into destructive behaviors in their teen years.

If your family goes to the homecoming game in the next four years, point out the fifth-grade "couples," so that you can talk to your child about the situation when you are back home. Explain that there are better ways to have fun at homecoming than being tied down to one child of the opposite sex. Be sure the boys are aware of how much those mums would cost them—and that it will not be an expense paid by parents.

Begin in advance to plan something special for your child and his or her friends. For example, a group of friends of both sexes could all sit together and go out for pizza before or after the game. If video games are available at the pizza restaurant, those boys could play for a long time on the money they saved by not buying mums.

As the time approaches, let your child know that going to the game "with a date" is not an option. Discuss this in an upbeat manner with more emphasis on the alternate plans.

I am a stay-at-home mom. My children are five, four, and two. Although I have a business degree that I plan to use someday, I would not trade these years with my children. However, I'm concerned about the subtle message I'm sending my son and my daughters. Will my son expect all women to be fulltime moms and will my daughters fail to realize that they need a career, even if they plan to put it on hold for a few years?

Good for you for making the sacrifice to stay home for a few years. It's a big decision that must be made by each couple based on their unique circumstances. Many families find that the investment

152

of those years away from a career do pay off for the children. And that the harm to the mother's career is not as big an issue as they had thought.

Your children need to see you active in more than changing diapers and cleaning up messes. Many stay-at-home moms volunteer where they have a passion in something not connected to their child-rearing duties. You might find a way to use your business degree in volunteer work. That not only allows your children to see you as more than a mom, but those volunteer roles look good on your resume when you decide later to work outside the home.

Another way to teach your children gender equality is to teach all of them to do all types of work in the home. If you always send your son out with the trash and let the girls help in the kitchen, you teach them that jobs are gender specific. It's good to prepare each child to do every job associated with home maintenance, meal preparation, and laundry. When they leave for college—a time that seems far off right now—they will be prepared to survive on their own.

PARENT GOALS FOR THIS STAGE

- Decide in advance your position about your child's relationship with the opposite sex.
- Remove your own prejudices. Determine that you will be open to all interests for all children.
- If possible, find other parents who will stand with you.
- Inform grandparents and other relatives of your position.
- Expose your child to people who have non-traditional careers and interests for their gender.

ACTION TO EMPOWER

I will empower my child by . . .
(list one way you will encourage your child to play outside traditional gender roles).

_____

_____

_____

_____

_____

_____

Section 7: Independence

It is not what you do for your children, but what you have taught them to do for themselves that will make them successful human beings.
Ann Landers

Imagine your children as young adults living on their own in an apartment. Will they have the skills to run their household, prepare meals, and take care of themselves? Will they know how to manage their finances? The tasks—most of which you perform now—will be their responsibility. You cannot teach them all they need to know in the last few months before they leave home. The sooner you begin, the easier the transition will be when the time comes.

That Dreaded Word: Chores

Our house is clean enough to be healthy,
and dirty enough to be happy.
Author Unknown

Goals for Age Eighteen

- Knows how to care for all aspects of a home.
- Is motivated to care for a home.
- Learns the joy of working "as though you were working for the Lord."[40]
- Knows the difference between keeping a home clean enough to enjoy and obsessing over cleanliness.

I'm Bored

Six-year-old Madison sat on the floor, looking at a children's magazine. A dust cloth lay on the floor beside her.

Laura walked into the family room and took a deep breath before speaking. "Madison, you're not dusting. Are you trying to make the job last all morning?"

"I got tired."

"Tired. Why? You haven't done anything all morning except carry that dust cloth from the laundry room to its resting place there on the floor. Get busy."

Madison looked at the magazine one last time and put it in the basket. "I'm bored."

"Bored? I don't understand. You always help with the chores on Saturday mornings. Now, you are making one job last forever. Just get up and get to work." Laura turned and left the room.

Madison picked up the dust cloth and took coasters, the remote, and a magazine off the table. With little enthusiasm, she began to dust the end table.

Seven-year-old Ryan walked through the family room, pulling the vacuum. "Hey, Maddy. What're you doing? I vacuumed the whole house while you just sat there."

"You get to do all the good stuff. I hate dusting."

"I'm older. You probably couldn't handle the vacuum. I'm heading outside to play baseball. We could use your fielding—if you ever finish in here."

Madison set the items back on the table and moved over to the coffee table. *Ugh. Everybody treats me like a baby. I've been dusting since I was two. But maybe I really can't handle the vacuum—like Ryan says.*

Shake Up the Chore Assignment

Madison correctly articulates why she is in a slump about her chore. She's been dusting since she was two. Though she might not enjoy vacuuming any more than dusting, it would be a change and a challenge.

157

Parents easily fall into the same pattern that Laura is following. She assigned an appropriate chore for Madison when she was two and never changed it.

Look at the situation from Madison's viewpoint.

- The job offers no challenge. She mastered it years ago.
- The job was exciting when her mom first handed her a dust cloth at age two. Now, it's not.
- She sees an older brother with a job that requires more skill.
- Her overall view of the situation is that she has a baby-ish, boring job, while her brother, only a year older, has an interesting job.

There are many creative ways to stir up the chore list. I suggest posting a list every Saturday morning. Let all the children pick the ones they will do for the week. They can take turns being the first to choose. Chores will rotate, allowing each child to learn all household jobs. At ages six and seven, the chores do not need to be differentiated by age. Only if there is a great age difference would it be appropriate for some chores to be restricted to the older children. Dollie Freeman has a list of chores on her website that are appropriate for preschoolers and toddlers. She offers it in printable format so it can be posted on a fridge.[41]

Branch out in what you allow your children to do. By the time children start school, they should be able to fold linens, dry-mop hard floors and wet-mop floors with supervision. Let them take turns vacuuming. And yes, they can clean bathrooms. They can unload the dishwasher, even if they have to stack some items on the counter to be put away by a parent. Understand that they may not do the chores to your standards in the beginning. It takes time to become proficient.

Encouragement is important. Begin by allowing them to evaluate their job. Ask them how they think they did. At this age, the question can be as simple as, "Before I check your work, tell me—

158

did you do super good, kinda good, or not so good?" It's amazing how often kids nail it just the same as your evaluation.

Remember that you shouldn't expect perfection as they learn, but instead, celebrate improvement.

But My Friend Is Waiting

The doorbell rang. Six-year-old Ethan peeked out the window, saw his friend, and opened the door. "Hi, Daniel."

"Hey. Can you play?"

Ethan looked down at Daniel's skateboard. "Sure. Come in. I'll get my board and tell Mom."

Daniel set his skateboard by the door.

Ethan's mom, Amber, peeked out of the kitchen. "Hi, Daniel. What's up?"

"I'm skateboarding and want Ethan to come with me."

"I am not sure he's ready to play. Let me check."

Amber started down the hall just as Ethan came out of his room, carrying his skateboard.

"Oh hi, Mom. Daniel wants me to play."

Amber motioned Daniel back into his room. "I need to check your room. Your job this morning was to clean it and put away everything."

"Uh, I didn't finish. I can do it when I get back."

"No. I'm sorry. The deal is that Saturday morning chores are done first—before you play. I can see things are not picked up. Are you telling me it's not clean either?

"Ah, Mom. I can do it later. Daniel's waiting."

"How long will it take you to get the job done? You can tell Daniel so he'll know when to come back."

"Mom. That's not fair. Daniel's already here."

"Ethan, you went to your room two hours ago to clean it and

159

put things away. Now go tell Daniel when you'll be ready."

Ethan dropped his skateboard and walked toward the front of the house like someone about to face a firing squad. "Daniel," he said, "it'll be an hour before I can come outside. My mom is making me clean my room first. I'll come to your house when I finish."

"Okay, see you later."

Of course, Ethan failed to tell Daniel that he'd had all morning to do a simple cleaning job. Amber would let that omission slide since he didn't dishonor her to his friend. They dealt with that behavior last month. It was always something.

She would need to check on him in about fifteen minutes to see that he was doing a good job. With the pressure of a friend waiting to play, it would be tempting to slack off.

Chores First, Then Play

Amber handled a situation that parents face frequently. It may be skateboarding at six, but at sixteen the teen could miss a trip to the mall because he didn't do his Saturday chores. It is better to set the precedent now—Saturday chores need to be completed before weekend play begins.

If something big is planned for Saturday, such as a day trip with a friend's family, Amber will remind Ethan that he must complete his Saturday chores by bedtime on Friday. If he doesn't, he will have to call his friend and cancel.

This seems harsh, but children will try to work the system to their advantage. It's easy to use the friend standing at the door to pressure parents to let it go "just this one time."

FOUNDATIONS FOR THIS STAGE

- Children need to do chores, not only to learn the skills but to contribute to the family.
- Children at this age like the challenge of learning new jobs.
- Variety in assignments makes the work easier.
- When children tackle a new chore, they must be allowed time to learn before they are expected to do it well.
- Chores need deadlines for completion. If he has something planned close to the deadline, it is up to the child to complete them ahead of time.
- Respect your child by talking about his incomplete chores in private rather than in front of friends. If he can't play because he hasn't done his chores, he should be the one to tell his friend.
- Listen to the explanation and be sure your child does not dishonor you by saying you are mean or by using other accusatory words.

FAQs

I have one child who does his chores with enthusiasm. He does a great job, whatever his assignment, and does it with a good attitude. The other child procrastinates, complains, and does the bare minimum when she finally decides to work. How can I change her attitude and commitment to chores?

Ah, the difference between siblings . . . doesn't it make life interesting? No doubt, your daughter shines in some places where your son needs improvement. There are three things to consider:

- Despite your daughter's resistance to work, make sure

you do not lighten her load or expect less of her. Continue to teach each of them how the job looks when it's done correctly. If she chooses to do a sloppy job, make her do it over.

- Ignore her complaining. She would love to argue with you instead of doing her work. Don't let her pull you into debates. Rather than talk about the sloppy job she did mopping the kitchen, firmly tell her that she must redo it before she can do anything else. Hand her the mop and walk away.

- As much as possible, separate your children when they are working. If the good-natured child is in the other end of the house, he won't have to listen to his contentious sister. He might even finish his chores and go outside, away from the complaining.

Keep in mind that you are training your children for the day they will leave home. It's about more than getting the work done.

The best way to handle the chores is

- Assign the chore.
- Be sure your children have the tools and instructions.
- Remind them to call you for inspection and walk away.
- After you inspect the job, dismiss them with praise for a job well done, or tell them to bring it up to the required standards—and walk away again.

Should I pay my kids for the chores they do? We aren't sure how chores and allowances are connected.

I suggest a three-tier system for chores and pay.[42]

- Self-Maintenance Chores: Every child is responsible for his own messes and maintenance. A toddler can learn where his dirty clothes go and wipe up spills. A preschooler can sort clothes and bring them to the laundry room. An early-elementary child can do a load of laundry, complete from dirty to folded in a drawer. A child at any of these ages should put away what he gets out, whether it's food, toys, or clothes. These are not paid jobs, but clean-up-what-you-mess-up jobs.

- Family Chores: Each family member should contribute to the general work of the household. You might assign two chores for the week. For example, a six-year-old might unload the dishwasher as needed and take out the trash. The weekly chore would be cleaning the bathroom at the end of the week. The chores rotate depending on what each child chooses. These are not paid jobs. They are responsibilities that go with being in the family. An allowance is also part of being in the family and is a tool for teaching money management. These two are not connected.

- Extra Chores: Paying for extra jobs is a good way to teach about work. Post a list of chores with the pay associated with them. Pay is low for learners and higher as competency increases.[43] These opportunities allow kids to save for big items such as video game consoles. It's better for kids to work and save for an Xbox rather than you having to dish out several hundred dollars without your child learning the connection between work and money.

PARENT GOALS FOR THIS STAGE

- Organize the household-chore system. See Appendix: Managing Chore Assignments for a sample sign-up sheet and a link to an article about a system for chores.
- Rotate sign-ups so that each child has opportunities to learn all chores. Include adults in the rotation.

- Stick to your guns. Do not allow your children to talk you into letting them off the hook "just this one time." Once you let down the boundary, they will keep pushing for you to do it again.
- In the beginning, accept imperfection in chores, but encourage your children to seek improvement.

ACTION TO EMPOWER

I will empower my child by . . .
(describe a new chore or decision about a chore you will turn over to your child).

_____

_____

_____

_____

_____

_____

Kitchen Lessons

The shared meal is no small thing. It is a foundation of family life, the place where our children learn the art of conversation and acquire the habits of civilization: sharing, listening, taking turns, navigating differences, arguing without offending.
Michael Pollan

Goals for Age Eighteen

- Knows how to choose and prepare healthy food.
- Makes healthy choices most of the time.
- Is confident enough about food choices to make healthy choices around peers but can go with the flow when necessary.
- Enjoys food preparation.

Grandmothers: Ice Cream for Babies

Christina and her sister-in-law Meagan carried dishes to the kitchen. They insisted that the rest of the family continue to visit around the table while they got dessert. Christina let Granna and Pops entertain six-month-old Ava.

Megan set down the stack of plates. "Thanks for a delicious meal. You're a great cook."

"I like having the family together," Christina said. "Your mom and dad seemed to enjoy themselves. I'm glad they were able to be here too."

After they cleared the last of the dishes, Christina got out some ice cream. "I didn't do anything for dessert. I hope ice cream is okay. Why don't you check and see if everyone wants some."

Meagan returned to the dining room to get a count. Her mother said, "Count me in and put in an extra scoop. I'll share with Ava."

"Mom, I don't think Christina lets Ava have ice cream yet."

"What do you mean? We mustn't leave her out."

"I'll ask."

Megan watched Christina dipping ice cream. "It looks so good, but I'm going to pass, so just four bowls from in there. And you are about to face a tiger grandma. Mom thinks Ava needs ice cream."

Christina chuckled and shook her head. "Uh-oh. Thanks for the heads up."

Christina and Megan carried the bowls to the table. Christina handed half of a banana to Ava. "Here you go, sweetie."

Ava loved bananas. It would be all over her face by the time she finished, but she enjoyed the independence of feeding herself.

"Christina, don't give that baby a banana while we're all eating ice cream. That's mean. I'll be glad to feed her ice cream out of my bowl."

Christina took a deep breath. "Linda, we're not ready for Ava to have ice cream."

"Why not? She'll love it."

Michael, Christina's husband, patted his mom's hand. "Mom, there'll be time enough for ice cream. Ava's doctor recommended we wait, at least until she's one, maybe longer."

"You kids have all these new-fangled ideas about raising children. You started eating ice cream about the time you could sit up in your high chair."

"Maybe that's why I love sugar so much. Look at this gut. I fight it all the time."

"That's because you're behind a desk eight hours a day. How about just one spoonful?"

"No, Mom. Look. She's enjoying her banana."

Christina appreciated her husband getting into the discussion, but she couldn't help adding her reasons. "Linda, the doctor said we run the risk of causing food allergies if we let her have ice cream before she's one. He also said the earlier we let kids eat refined sugar and flour, the more likely they'll have weight problems. I know you don't want that for Ava."

Linda stuck out her lower lip in a pretend pout. "Well, okay. You're denying Granna the joy of feeding her grandbaby yummy ice cream. But promise me you'll invite me over for her first ice cream."

Christina laughed. "You'll be the first to know, I promise. In fact, let's just make a date for her birthday party. Her cake will put her on a sugar high. We might as well top it off with ice cream."

Saying No to Ice Cream

Michael and Christina are right to insist that his mother not feed Ava ice cream. Most health professionals recommend introducing cow's milk after age one.[44] The likelihood that the child will develop an allergy to milk goes down after that age. There is the additional food issue of refined sugar and flour.

Many parents limit the amount of sugar their children eat at any age. Sugar consumption is a big problem in our country. You

167

only need to read labels to realize it's in foods that don't seem to need sugar.

I will leave it to the health professionals to determine the best course of action. However, parents need to be aware of the issue and ask their child's physician.

Your children will be inundated with sugary foods as they get older. However, the habits that you begin early will be with them for life. Since there's a strong possibility of long-term health issues associated with sugar, the safe choice is to limit sugar[45] at an early age. Fresh fruit is an excellent choice for dessert.

As far as the introduction of foods, there is continued debate about the right time. Since the research is ongoing, check with your health professional and do your own research regarding this issue.

Veggies as Appetizers

Have you watched toddlers chase oat cereal O's around on their highchair tray? I used the cereal to keep my kids occupied in restaurants, or while I prepared a meal. The cereal is healthier than some choices, but consider this scene for an example of extreme health—baby health to the max:

While Sarah chopped veggies for the soup she was making, Daniel, age three, sat in his highchair, eating frozen mixed-vegetable cubes from a plastic bowl.

Daniel picked up a piece of carrot and showed it to his mom. "What's this?"

Sarah laughed, "That doesn't look like a carrot, does it Danny?" She held up a whole carrot. "This is what carrots look like before someone chops them into little pieces. Do you want to taste the big carrot?"

Daniel clapped his hands. "Yes."

Sarah grated off a piece of carrot. "Here you go. Then try

yours. See if they taste alike."

Daniel tasted both carrots. "Mine's cold."

"That's because it's been in the freezer. Putting food in the freezer makes it as cold as ice. Then we call it *frozen*.

Sarah picked up a stack of fresh green beans. "Do you have a green bean on your tray?'

Daniel looked. He found one green bean and held it up for his mom to see.

"Do you want to try one of my green beans?" Sarah held up a fresh whole one.

"It's long."

"I can cut it into short pieces."

"No. I want it whole."

"Daniel, I'm going to cut it into little pieces so you won't choke on it. When you are a little older, you can have a whole one."

"I want it whole." Daniel banged his feet on the foot rest.

"Daniel, stop that, or I'll make you get down before you finish your snack."

Daniel banged his feet one more time before he complied.

Sarah chose to ignore his little act of defiance. She put two tiny slices of raw green beans on his tray. As she continued making soup, she asked him to name all the veggies he could find on his tray.

"Carrots, beans, uh, round beans, corn."

"The little round green ones are called *peas*."

Daniel pointed to each one. "Carrots, beans, peas, corn."

"High five, big guy. You named them all."

Sarah and Daniel did a high five, and Daniel got tickled. For some reason, he thought it would be funny to dump the few remaining veggies on the floor.

"Oops, looks like you're finished. Let me help you down. Pick up the veggies and put them in the trash."

Daniel protested that he wasn't ready to get down, but Sarah told him that his snack was over because he was playing with his food.

Take Advantage of Time before Dinner

Although Daniel was not starving while Sarah prepared dinner, activity in the kitchen made him anticipate a meal, leave his toys behind, and become restless. When he stood on the kitchen floor, his view included the cabinet drawers and his mother's knees.

Putting Daniel in a highchair served three purposes. He could see what she was doing, which entertained him. She fed him a light healthy snack that kept him from being fussy while he waited for dinner. It also gave her an opportunity to teach him about food.

Sarah used the time to teach the names of the veggies. She talked about what *frozen* means. She reminded him that he must use good manners at the table and not play with his food.

FOUNDATIONS FOR THIS STAGE

- Healthy eating is a way of glorifying God. He gave us an awesome body, and it is up to us to take care of it. Teach your children that they are caring for God's temple[46] when they treat their bodies well.
- Begun early, food habits stay with your children for a lifetime.
- Focus conversations about food on the positive rather than the negative. Eating disorders can begin at this age, when parents are obsessive about food and eating habits.

- Check with a health professional about when to introduce foods, including cow's milk, in your child's diet. Introducing a food too early can cause allergies.
- Children are restless and need attention in the time before a meal. Feed your children raw vegetables while you prep a meal—a way to get extra veggies in their diets.
- A plate of raw veggies, sometimes called a "finger salad" is especially appealing before meals. Even teens often eat raw veggies if they're available as appetizers.
- Both parents should decide in advance on issues related to feeding their children. Then they can present a united front to relatives and friends who offer less healthy foods.
- Allow your children to help with food purchasing and meal preparation. They will be more interested in eating what they helped choose and prepare.

FAQs

I remember sitting on the countertop, helping my mother bake cookies. I don't cook desserts as often as my mother did. How can I get my three-year-old son involved in food preparation? Is he too young to help in the kitchen?

Many in previous generations thought love came wrapped in sugar. Today, we can show our families we love them by serving them healthy foods. You are on the right track. Congratulations for taking a big step toward your family's health.

A three-year-old can help with food prep in many ways. Let's start at the beginning and follow a toddler through the entire process.

- While making out a grocery list, have him help you check supplies in the kitchen.
- At the store, give him his own "list." His list might consist of a page with taped-on labels from food containers, such as his favorite cereal, milk, and a frozen pizza (yes, there are healthy pizzas in the freezer). The three items listed above can be seen from a three-year-old's level. As you go through the store, looking for the items on his list will keep him occupied.
- Back home, he can put away much of the food. A favorite job at this age will be to wash the produce and set it on a towel to drain. You may need an additional towel on the floor to catch the splashes. This can become a rollicking fun job at his age.
- With patience on your part, he can learn to crack eggs.
- He can measure ingredients, stir batter, and knead dough. The only functions he should not do is anything that involves heat or knives. And yes, he can clean up the messes he'll make.
- He can set the table. If you are concerned for your breakable dishes, begin with silverware and napkins. I often used plastic dishes while my children were learning. Then we made a big deal out of graduating to real plates.

There will be mishaps, but if you are patient enough to involve your child in the preparation of meals, he will become enthusiastic about foods. And meals prepared at home can be healthier than those eaten out.

My four-year-old has gotten picky about what she eats. Previously, she ate everything I offered her. Now she has narrowed her choices. I'm afraid she's not getting

enough healthy food. Sometimes, she leaves the table having eaten nothing. Thirty minutes later she says she's hungry.

Kids go through stages of rejecting foods. Part of this stems from growing independence. She realizes she has some control over what she eats. If it is power that she seeks, empower her by giving her choices. (Do you want your carrots on this side of your plate or this side?)

- Unless you make an issue of food during this stage, it is just that—a stage. It will pass.
- Put a small amount (1–2 tablespoons) of every food on her plate. If she serves her own plate, allow her to put the amount she chooses, even if it's tiny.
- Use the "one taste" rule. She must have a taste of everything on her plate. Again, if the taste is so small you can't imagine that she even feels it in her mouth, let it go. As she gets over this initial stage of rebellion, you can set certain amounts that must be eaten (such as two green beans or half of her "finger salad"). Despite our best efforts, kids may have some foods they never like. As much as I wanted them to like meatloaf, neither of my kids ever got past the one-taste stage. But then, how healthy is meatloaf, anyway?
- Don't prepare special foods for her. I had a rule for my own children. I'm not sure it was the right thing to do, but it worked for us. I allowed them to supplement certain meals with a peanut butter sandwich (no jam or honey). They prepared the sandwich, so that my meal was not disturbed. They could make the sandwich only after they had tasted every food on their plates. There was never another choice—only peanut butter and whole-wheat bread.
- Have your child ask permission to leave the table (May I

be excused?). Make sure she understands that when she leaves the table, she's finished eating until the next meal or scheduled snack. She may claim she's starving thirty minutes after leaving the table. Acknowledge her pain, but make her wait.

- There is an exception to the above rule. When we had company—and that was about the only time we had dessert—I allowed my children to leave the table and come back for dessert. Adults tend to linger over a meal longer than a child can be expected to sit.
- As hard as it is, keep in mind that your child will not starve by missing a meal.

If you face your child's need for independence with a no-nonsense attitude—few rules and little talk—eating problems are unlikely to develop. The one thing you must not do is make food and meals a battleground. You could be setting your child up for a lifetime of eating issues.

You may have grown up in a home where refusal to eat was treated differently than these suggestions. If you choose to face the problem as I have suggested, you may need to explain your stand with her grandparents. Hang tough, but with grace.

PARENT GOALS FOR THIS STAGE

- Learn about good food habits that you want to teach your children.
- Talk to your children's doctor. Many have excellent re-sources to help parents choose and prepare good food.
- Face your own food issues so you will not pass them to your children.
- Decide in advance what you will say and how you will say it when friends and family try to sabotage your plan

174

for feeding your children.

- Experiment with different foods. Make the experimentation a fun game. Involve your children in choosing new foods.
- Plan for the time before a meal when you're tired, your children are tired and hungry, and you need to focus on getting a meal on the table.

ACTION TO EMPOWER

I will empower my child by . . .
(choose one part of a meal that your child can make a healthy choice for the menu).

_____

_____

_____

_____

_____

_____

My Body: Owner's Manual

Don't you realize that your body is the temple of the Holy Spirit,
who lives in you and was given to you by God?
1 Corinthians 6:19

Goals for Age Eighteen

- Understands the sanctity of one's body.
- Knows how to respond to inappropriate physical advances.
- Knows and practices regular hygiene and grooming.
- Is comfortable asking for information about private issues.

Bathtime Lessons

"Look, Mommy—waves." Four-year-old Nicholas pushed to the back of the tub to create another wave.

Amanda heard a splash as she turned from the vanity. "Nicholas, what are you doing?"

"Making waves."

About that time water sloshed over the edge of the tub onto the bathroom floor. "Nicholas Caden, stop it this minute. It's time to finish your bath and get out." Amanda laid an extra towel on the floor to absorb the water. "Put soap on your wash cloth and let me see you scrub."

Nicholas began to wash his tummy. "See? Clean tummy."

"Yes, it is, Nicholas. How about the rest of you? May I wash your back?"

Nicholas gave his mom the wash cloth and soap.

She scrubbed his back and arms and handed him the soapy wash cloth. "Now, let me see you wash between your legs. That's private, so you need to be the one to do it."

Nicholas stood on his knees in the tub to wash his genitals and buttocks.

"That's good. Now sit down and wash between your toes. Nick, do you remember that I told you that all the area between your legs is private, and you must not let other people touch it or see it? That's why you don't run around the house without shorts on."

Amanda put the soap in its dish. "There might be a reason a doctor would need to look at it, and that would be okay. But you should not show your penis to friends or strangers. Do you understand?"

"Yes. I'm ready to get out." Nicholas stood and stepped onto the bath mat.

Amanda wrapped him in a towel and gave him a big hug as she dried his back. "Can you dry the rest of you and get into your PJs? Then we need to get your teeth brushed. I'll be back in a minute."

After he finished drying and putting on his pajamas, Nicholas got his toothbrush loaded and turned over the hourglass to time his brushing. When he finished, he rinsed his toothbrush and tapped out the water on the edge of the lavatory. He got more water on the brush and tapped harder and harder until water was flying everywhere.

Amanda walked back into the bathroom just as the water was running down the mirror. "Nicholas, stop. Let me finish brushing your teeth before you clean up your mess." She did a final job on Nicholas' teeth and handed him the toothbrush. "Put this away and get that hand towel. Dry everything you can reach. I think there's water on the floor. Move your step stool and dry there too."

Squatted, Amanda was eye level with Nicholas. "Nick, the bathroom is not the place to splash water. Save that for the swimming pool or the yard. Don't do it again, or you'll be in timeout in your room. Do you understand?"

"Yes ma'am"

"Okay, after you clean up your mess, go choose a book, and I'll meet you on the sofa."

Teaching Care for and Respect of Body

Amanda is teaching Nicholas important self-care skills. Because he's only four, she is either in the bathroom with him or close by. He's allowed to play in the water as long as he doesn't make a mess. She still scrubs his back and supervises the rest of his washing.

She talks to him occasionally about privacy. Bath time is a good opportunity to do that while she also teaches him to bathe his own genital area. Sometimes, she can include discussions about strangers and friends who might breach his privacy. She'll make sure he knows to tell someone if that ever happens.

By discussing this matter casually, Amanda takes away the stigma of talking about sensitive issues. He is more likely to come to her with his concerns in the future. It may seem early to think about sexual concerns, but at some point they will need to discuss the onset of puberty, society's push for premarital sex, and sexually transmitted diseases (STD's). Right now, she's preparing him for open, comfortable talks when that time comes.

In addition to teaching about hygiene, she is also helping him develop good habits. She established a routine for getting ready for bed that included bathing, brushing teeth, and winding down with a story.

A Fit Family

"Everybody gets two water bottles," Dad said. "Mom and I will carry the extras. Come pick out energy bars for your backpack. Lunch goes in my load." Bryson went to the fridge to get the lunch that Mom packed the night before.

Three-year-old Josh held up his plastic Superman. "Can he go?"

Bryson took the toy and hefted it as if to check its weight. "Think you can handle the extra weight in your pack?"

"Sure, Dad."

"Okay, he gets to go hiking too."

"Aw, Dad. He won't hike. He's gonna ride in my backpack."

"Oh yeah, right. I forgot."

Eight-year-old Eli looked up from packing. "Where's Mom? I hope she's bringing chips."

Dad cuffed Eli on the shoulder. "Nice try, Son. When we hike, we need nutrient-dense food. Chips don't qualify."

"Oh all right. What's in our lunch?"

"I didn't even look before I put it in my pack. I guess we'll both be surprised. But knowing your mom, it'll be healthy."

Kimberly came into the kitchen and grabbed energy bars for her backpack. She looked at Keith. "You packed our lunch?"

Yes. The kids each have two waters and two energy bars. They have sunglasses. Do you have the sunscreen? What else?"

179

"I have the sunscreen, the first aid kit, and my cell phone."

Eli slung his backpack over his shoulder. "I'm ready. Oh, which trail are we hiking this time?"

Dad pulled a paper out of his pocket. "I downloaded a map of the trails from the Caprock Canyon website. I thought we might hike up to the scenic overlook on the John Haynes Ridge. I think there's room there to have our picnic. In a couple of years, we'll go all the way to the Fern Cave. You guys need to be a little older before we tackle that. We can hike a little way on the ridge before we start back down. How does that sound?"

Eli nodded. "That's cool."

Josh picked up his backpack. "I want to see the buffaloes."

"Maybe they'll be near the road this time." Dad zipped his backpack and stood up. "Okay, let's load up."

The family threw their stuff in the back of the van. Josh grabbed his backpack and dug around. "Wait. Superman rides with me."

The family climbed in and buckled up. Dad looked around to check that everyone was belted as he backed out of the drive. "We're off to the canyons."

Focus on Fitness

Keith and Kimberly make fitness a priority for their family. Hikes, soccer in the backyard, and camping trips become their family fun rather than television and video games. They get the family outside as much as possible.

Not only does the entire family benefit from the physical exercise, but they enjoy being together in God's creation.

Keith and Kimberly teach their kids what foods are good fuel for their bodies. They pack nutritious lunches and snacks for their hike and emphasize good nutrition in their at-home meals.

They will have a devotional when they reach the scenic overlook. If there isn't cell service to use her app, Kimberly has a small Bible tucked in her backpack. Imagine the joy of sitting on the canyon ridge overlooking God's handiwork as they listen to God's words to Job:

Where were you when I laid the foundations of the earth? Tell Me, if you have understanding. Who determined its measurements? Surely you know! Or who stretched the line upon it? To what were its foundations fastened? Or who laid its cornerstone, when the morning stars sang together, and all the sons of God shouted for joy?[47]

FOUNDATIONS FOR THIS STAGE

- At this age, a parent should be nearby during baths, for both instruction and safety.
- As soon as they are able, children should wash their own genital areas.
- Use bath time to discuss the importance of keeping the "private areas" of their bodies private.
- Most children cannot do an adequate job of brushing their teeth until around age seven. They can practice and let a parent finish the job.
- When families do physical and outdoor activities together, the children learn health habits that last a lifetime.
- The concept that "food is fuel" is applicable when a family is doing physical activities.
- God's creation is a great place to have fun, bond with family, and get to know the Creator.

FAQs

I have one child who loves the outdoors, but my five-year-old daughter hates physical activity and being outside. She would much rather play with her dolls and read books. What can I do to increase her enthusiasm about outdoor activities?

Check first to be sure she's comfortable when she's outside. Some children are naturally more sensitive to heat, pollen, and sun. They need things like good shoes, clothes appropriate to the season, and sunscreen. They may need allergy medication. All these precautions will make being outdoors a better experience.

Get her involved in preparing for the outdoor adventures, whether a camping trip or a backyard picnic. If she prepares or packs some of the food, she'll want to be on hand when the family raves about it.

Let her plan some of the activities. For instance, she may have a book she wants the family to read by flashlight in the tent. Allow her to take along a sketchbook and colored pencils to draw what she observes in the wild. And of course, her favorite doll should go camping too. Make a big deal of the doll's participation.

We often make the mistake of thinking that only certain activities are appropriate for outside fun. Especially if she has a big brother, those activities may include putting yucky worms on a hook or other disgusting activities that are the usual fare of camping trips. As the two of you think outside the box, perhaps you will find fun things for her to do when the family is outside.

There are many activities you can do together. Take a nature walk and record what you see with drawings, photos, or journal entries. Bring a favorite book and stretch out on a blanket to read. Put some distance between you and the fishermen (they'll protest if you disturb the water) and learn to skip rocks.

I work fulltime and am tired at night. The biggest hassle I face each night is getting my children ready for bed. I don't want to wish away my children's lives, but it will be such a relief when they can take care of bed time by themselves. Any suggestions on how to make it run more efficiently?

One of the key words to think about in child-rearing is *empowerment*. That means you let your children do what they're capable of doing as soon as they're able. For example, I'm sure you agree that your children should be empowered to get ready for bed alone.

I found that the hardest part for me (I also worked fulltime and was tired at night.) was keeping our family on a schedule.

Some people complain that a schedule is too rigid and makes for unhappy children. That's not true.

Children thrive within boundaries. My children knew I was going to begin reading to them about fifteen minutes before eight. If they messed around and weren't ready, they missed some of the story. That sounds mean, but rarely did they fail to get to the sofa on time.

If my kids were ready for our story on time, they got a reward when they went to bed. They could read or look at a picture book for thirty minutes before lights-out. By being on time, they got to read for an extra thirty minutes. It was a no-brainer that they wanted to earn that privilege.

Teach your children the steps for getting ready for bed. Make it easy by having everything accessible. The place where they put their dirty clothes should be convenient. Teach them to hang up towels by making them go back and do it if they throw them on the floor. The time comes out of their reading time. Have a step stool so they can reach to turn on the water. Give each child a place to keep his or her toothpaste and toothbrush.

If you are having difficulty getting them to clean up the bathroom, ask them to call you for "inspection." For extra motivation, give smiley face stickers for a neat bathroom.

As you work to train them, more and more you will be able to step out of the bathroom to do other things. The time you spend supervising will gradually decrease until they are doing it on their own. Ample praise for their accomplishments increases their desire to be responsible.

PARENT GOALS FOR THIS STAGE

- If possible, commit to physical activities as a family every weekend.
- Educate yourself about healthy food to take on outdoor excursions. There is ample information available in bookstores and on the Internet.
- Create a time schedule for bath time and story time. Discuss the schedule and the consequence for not following it. The consequence could be starting the bedtime ritual earlier the next night.
- Make the bathroom as kid-friendly as possible so they can reach things and have a place to put their dirty clothes, towels, and toiletries.

ACTION TO EMPOWER

I will empower my child by . . .
(describe a way your child can participate to plan a family outing).

_____

_____

_____

_____

_____

_____

Substance Abuse Lessons for Preschoolers

Healthy communication at home is the best means
of setting your children down the path to a promising
future free of alcohol and drug abuse.
Glenn Williams, D.Min.

Goals for Age Eighteen

- Views one's body as the temple of God[48] to be treated with care.
- Knows how to abstain from alcohol with grace or, when of legal age, how to drink responsibly.
- Uses over-the-counter and prescription drugs only as needed after healthy lifestyle methods prove insufficient.
- Is comfortable discussing the topics of alcohol and drugs with parents or other responsible adult advisers.

Adult Beverages

Five-year-old Jake and his dad pitched a baseball back and forth as his mom came out of the house. She set a tray on the patio table. "Time for a break, guys."

Jake came to the table and looked at what was on the tray. "Which drink is mine?" He grabbed a Clementine orange and a handful of almonds.

Mom picked up a stainless water bottle. "There's water in here. Or you can have the apple Izze—special treat."

She tousled Jake's damp hair. "You've been playing hard. You may want them both." She carried a wine cooler and some rice crackers to a chair in the shade.

Dad picked up some almonds and the can of beer before sprawling in a lounge chair. "That boy's wearing me out. I'm glad you came to my rescue."

"Dad?"

"Yes, Son."

"May I try your beer?"

"When you're an adult, yes. Not now. Beer and your mom's wine cooler are adult beverages. The law says you need to be twenty-one to drink alcohol."

"Why?"

"Your brain is still developing. Alcohol wouldn't be good for it,[49] and we want your brain to be the best it can be, right?"

"Sure, Dad. But you're drinking it."

"Adult brains are finished growing." Dad laughed. "I guess my brain's not going to get any better. It's safe to drink in moderation. Do you know what "in moderation" means?"

"No."

"We only drink when we sit and visit with each other or with friends. And then we do it slowly so our bodies don't get big jolts of alcohol."

"When I'm twenty-one, can I drink beer?"

"Yes, in fact I will take you out to eat and buy you a beer for your twenty-first birthday. By then, you'll know how to drink responsibly. Okay?

"Okay."

"It's a deal."

Teach Responsible Drinking by Example

Jake and his dad's conversation planted some seeds. In the coming years, there will be more discussions to further his understanding of responsible alcohol consumption.

His parents also modeled safe ways to enjoy alcoholic beverages. Jake observed several behaviors when he was on the patio with his parents.

- Drinking in moderation. They only had one drink each.
- Drinking in a social setting.
- Sipping drinks rather than guzzling them.
- No reference to "needing" a drink. Alcohol was not used "because I had a bad day."
- Eating food while drinking alcohol.

What children learn about how their parents enjoy adult beverages will influence how they will think about the use of other substances. Jake's dad mentioned the law, a point he will continue to teach until his son is twenty-one. That lesson also affects how Jake will view the use of illegal substances.

Note that Jake's dad gave him only a small amount of information about alcohol and drinking. He stopped to be sure that Jake knew what "in moderation" meant. One key to teaching our children facts is delivering information in small doses. Information overload causes children's and teens' ears to shut down.

188

Let's Take a Walk

"Emily," Kim said, "get your shoes, and let's go for a walk."

Six-year-old Emily ran to her bedroom in search of socks and shoes while Kim went to tell her husband they were leaving. Emily returned carrying her shoes.

"Em, go ahead and put them on. I'm not in that big a hurry."

Emily sat on the floor and pulled on her socks. "You said you had a headache." She tightened the Velcro closures and stood up.

"I do. That's why I want to go for a walk."

"Why don't you just take a pill? That's what Aunt Jillian does when she has a headache."

Kim held the door for Emily. As they walked down the steps, she sighed. "That might work, Emily, but I'd rather give my body a chance to get rid of the headache on its own."

Emily's brows knit together as her mom's statement soaked in. "Can it do that?"

"Sure. My headache is from sitting at the computer too long, so I just need to relax. Walking helps.

"It'd be easier just to take a pill." Emily pantomimed throwing a pill into her mouth.

"Do you know what a pain pill does?"

"Makes the headache go away?"

Yes. It does that by making us not feel the pain. If my head aches because I need to relax, I could still be tense and just not know. I'd rather go for a walk—especially with my daughter. Besides, I love getting outside in the world God created."

"Is it bad to take a pill for a headache?"

"No, it's not bad. I just think it's better to try relaxing first. If that doesn't work, I might take ibuprofen later.

"Mom, look at those flowers in Mrs. Smith's yard. May I pick one?"

"They're beautiful, aren't they? We need to leave them so

everyone can enjoy them. Mrs. Smith works in her yard several hours every day. I think that's her way of relaxing."

Emily laughed. "I bet she never has headaches."

"Probably not. If I had a garden like hers, I might stay outside all the time—and never get the inside work done."

A Healthy Way to Manage Pain

Kim teaches her daughter responsible use of legal drugs—over-the-counter and prescription. Kids notice if their parents reach for a pill for every little pain or mood swing. It's a short step for teens to go from legal to illegal drugs to ease pain, which may be physical or emotional. In many cases, teens who use alcohol (an illegal drug for teens) or other illegal drugs are attempting to ease their own pain from social inadequacy or failure to live up to perceived expectations.

Kim is modeling a healthy way to manage pain through physical exercise. There are other methods to handle tension and the resulting headaches. Relaxation techniques such as deep breathing is an example. Parents can include their children in these exercises, even though the children may not be tense.

Notice that Kim is not telling Emily that all medication is bad. She told her daughter that if a walk didn't cure her headache, she might take ibuprofen.

FOUNDATIONS FOR THIS STAGE

- Discussion of alcohol and other drugs should begin at an early age. A guideline for talking about any subject is to talk to our kids before their peers do.

- Alcohol should be used in social settings, always in moderation and never to relieve stress or pain.
- Before taking over-the-counter and prescription medication, try lifestyle changes to improve feelings and overall good health.
- If your family chooses to abstain from alcohol, you still need to discuss the subject with your kids. Include more than an admonition not to drink.

FAQs

My husband and I don't drink. If we teach our children about responsible drinking, aren't we condoning drinking? We would rather they not drink at all.

I congratulate you for standing strong for what you believe. However, it's important to prepare your children to face issues they will hear about from peers. If you don't instruct them, their peers and the media will do it for you. I am certain you'll not be happy with what they learn from those sources.

If all you tell your children is that alcohol is bad and to be avoided, they'll soon discover that yours is the minority opinion. By the time kids reach middle school, they question everything you've taught them. While there are good reasons for abstinence from alcohol, to your middle-schooler your belief will appear to be one of many outdated stances from another generation.

If you choose to give your preschoolers information about alcohol, let it be in response to some exposure in their environment. As an example, if you're at a family gathering and your children notice part of the group drinking something they don't recognize, they may ask about it.

That gives you the opportunity to tell them what alcohol is and one reason you choose not to drink. I heard a mother in a similar situation explain that she had a relative who misused alcohol and hurt the family by doing so. It's better to be specific in that way rather than using a general statement such as "it's wrong."

Unless your children ask, wait for this conversation until they're about to start school. Your children will hear other kindergartners talk about the alcohol their parents and older siblings drink. It's important to expose your kids to your values before they hear what others have to say.

The most important guideline I give parents who don't drink is to be open in answering questions and to be specific in your reasons for abstaining.

Another thing to consider: your children may decide to drink in adulthood, despite your efforts to teach abstinence. In that case, you will want them to know guidelines for responsible alcohol use.

As you talk to your kids, remember that small doses of information are more effective than information overload.

You've talked about over-the-counter (OTC) and prescription drugs and alcohol. What about the hard stuff? At what age and how much should I teach my preschooler?

Again, it's easy to do information overload. Is there an example of illegal drug use among your friends and family? If there is, your child may ask questions. Or worse, he or she may overhear comments by adults and be afraid to ask. In either situation, it would be good to give your young child small bits of information. You might say, "I know you heard the talk about Uncle Sammy being in jail. He used an illegal drug that affected his ability to drive his car. When he had a wreck, another person was hurt, and Uncle Sammy was arrested."

Pause so your child can process what he's hearing, then ask if he understands. "Now, Uncle Sammy's in jail waiting for a trial.

He's been using drugs for a couple of years and has gotten into a lot of trouble. Does that make sense out of what you heard in the kitchen? Do you have any questions?"

If your child has not been exposed to someone who uses illegal drugs, it might be best to wait until he's ready for elementary school. He will hear about drugs from classmates. As in other sensitive subjects, you will want to be the one who talks to him first.

PARENT GOALS FOR THIS STAGE

- If you drink, model responsible drinking for your children.
- Give your kids tidbits of information about drugs and alcohol rather than a lecture that covers the entire subject.
- Model the use of healthy ways to relieve pain and stress, such as physical exercise, healthy diet, and laughter.
- Avoid the use of alcohol "because I've had a bad day."

ACTION TO EMPOWER

I will empower my child by . . .
(give one way you will allow your child to lead the discussion about alcohol and drugs).

_____

_____

_____

_____

_____

_____

Section 8:
Endings and New Beginnings

Seven years is a long time in the life of a child, but when you look back, the years will feel like they have flown by. If you are like most parents, you wonder if you did enough. Did you listen well, comfort when comfort was needed, and guide back to the right path when your child veered off-track?

The good news is that God's grace and guidance allows us to raise reasonably well-adjusted children when our hearts are right and our intent is for good. If he didn't, none of us would make it.

About the time your children enter second grade, you reach a new stage. From now on, their peers play an increasing role in their lives. In the next few years (ages 7–11) you will build on what you taught your children, as they compare their family to other families.

As they enter middle school (ages 11–14), you need stamina. This is the stage when children test your ideas. If you know that in advance, you will understand that your child is not messed up— only testing the waters. That knowledge will help you weather the storm.

Finally, as your child enters high school, the rewards begin to show up. I say that with caution, because early high school offers plenty of opportunities for rebellion. If you laid the foundation, built on it, and allowed your children to test it, these years—especially the last two—are when they get to practice what they learned in the first sixteen years.

That freedom to practice is crucial. If you consider the facts, you would much rather your children practice—and fail sometimes—while they're still at home. At that point you become a consultant rather than a boss. You allow them to find solutions to the dilemmas they create.

This is the first of a series of books. The next one will be for parents of those delightful elementary-aged children. This will be a time of learning about the world outside their homes, meeting people who are different from the friends they had earlier, and finding their interests.

I wish you well as you parent. May joy be yours.

Appendix A:
Parenting BIG Ideas

There are some foundational concepts for good parenting. You came across these as you read this book. They transcend all stages of parenting. I group them together here for easy reference.

- Empowerment means not doing for your children anything they can do for themselves.
- Obedience to parents and other persons in positions of authority is the beginning of obedience to God.
- Children who understand their own worth in God's eyes are set free to love and serve others.
- Consistency is the way you tell children that you can be trusted.
- Courage comes to a child by taking small steps with a parent close by.
- Many rules at a young age mean fewer rules in adolescence.
- Family should be a place of jubilant rejoicing over success, tender encouragement after failure, and gentle correction of wrongdoings.
- Children have an amazing capacity to learn if someone takes the time to teach.

- To make any kind of change, three factors are needed: a reason, a plan, and an incentive.
- A key to teaching is to deliver information in small doses. Information overload causes hearing to shut down.
- A good guide for talking about any subject with our kids is to talk to them before their peers do.
- Our children's best first friends are the children of our friends, because they have the same values we do.
- Adults should have privileges children do not, thus making adulthood something to be desired.
- Children learn best in a structure that closely emulates the classical model.[50]
    1. Young children learn the facts.
    2. Middle-graders question the facts.
    3. Teens practice what they've learned.
- As parents teach their young children, they must also expect and prepare for the questioning that will come in middle school.
- The wise parent lets go enough in the last years for their teens at home to have freedom to practice what they've learned. This is the final stage for the foundation that you build now.

Appendix B:
Communication 101

Guidelines for Listening to
and Talking with Your Kids

- Listen more than you talk. Learn to hear what they say beneath their words.
- Never, never, never lecture. Sharing our vast wisdom may feel good, but who wants to hear a lecture about our misdeeds? I don't. Neither do our children. It's the most ineffective way *to attempt* to communicate with our children.
- Ask lots of questions—not digging-for-information questions, but *leading* questions. (So how do you think you should handle this? Now, what do you think you need to do?) This approach is a formidable empowering technique.
- Learn to be comfortable with silence. Right now, try this: Ask a question of the empty room where you sit and then time thirty seconds, which seems forever when you're waiting. But it is in those thirty seconds

(often less) that your children gather the courage to speak from their hearts.

- Use humor to diffuse strong emotions—not laughing at your child, but laughing at situations or at yourself.
- Openly discuss that two generations sometimes find talk difficult because they live in two different worlds. Plan together how you can get around that problem.
- Participate in their world and listen. I found out more about my children's worlds helping them with projects than I ever could have learned by asking questions. I discovered that guys (young and old) like "parallel communication" (side by side with no eye contact) that takes away the stigma of "a talk." I helped wax my teen son's car more than it ever needed so I could learn about his world.
- One thing I learned about children when they sat across from me in my counseling office: Children value their family more than they'll ever tell you openly. What they really want is *to know that you are in their corner.* Keep that thought in mind when the going gets tough.

Appendix C:
Managing Chore Assignments

When my children were young, I used a system for assigning chores. As they got older, I was less rigid about having them sign up. By that time, they picked what they liked best (or disliked least) and did it regularly. I occasionally had to prod a little, but I liked the idea of empowering them to do it without a chart.

Having a system in the beginning is good for several reasons:

- Everyone experiences all chores.
- There is fairness in the system. Without it, a lazy child devises ways to avoid participation.
- Everyone understands expectations.
- A system allows the child to plan when and how to get the work done—a powerful tool to empower children.

The mechanics of using a signup sheet has been explained in a blog on my website: "A *signup sheet* insures that everyone knows his or her responsibilities. With my children, I posted all common chores on Monday with a time when the chores were to be done. Each person had to sign up for a *during-the-week* chore (e.g.: unloading the dishwasher as needed) and two *Saturday* chores (e.g.: vacuuming). My children took turns being the one who was allowed to sign up first. I volunteered to be the last one to sign up for my chores."[51] If there had been a father in our home, it would have been important for him to participate also.

You will need to alter the sample chart to fit your family. I suggest using names for the children instead of "Child #1" because, who wants to be a *number two*? These chores are not comprehensive, only suggestions. The chart is on my website[52] so you may have it in electronic form and customize it for your family.

During the Week Chores: As Needed				
Beginning Date:	Dad	Mom	Child#1	Child#2
Unload Dishwasher				
Help with Meal Clean up				
Feed Pet/s				
Take out Trash				
Help with Meal Prep				

Weekly Chores: Before Saturday				
Vacuum				
Clean bathrooms				
Dust				
Sweep and Mop Hard Floors				
Wash, Dry, Fold Towels				
Poop-Scoop Yard				

Each family must devise personal guidelines for using the sign-up chart for chores. The following are only suggestions:

- All weekly chores must be done before weekend play begins—even if a friend is waiting or something is planned.
- Alternate who gets to choose chores first.
- Sign-up needs to be done by Sunday evening, or chores will be assigned.

- Require that each child, at some time, do each chore, even if it is not a favorite.
- As children get older, additional chores can be added, such as preparing a meal.
- If the family can afford the expense, additional "big" chores not on the list can be done for pay. That would necessitate an additional list of chores and the pay for doing them.

Appendix D:
Discipline and Punishment

Because God is the perfect father, we look to him to discover ways to parent our children. In light of that relationship, let's look at some key concepts regarding discipline.

Discipline is a word closely connected to *disciple* and *discipleship*. That connection makes it a good word. I want to be a disciple of Jesus. Although punishment is sometimes a necessity to carry out discipline. I'd rather avoid any situation in which God needs to punish me.

Another word key to this discussion is *consequences*. Often God allows the consequences of our disobedience to show us the right way. Hear what he said about the Israelites: *So I let them follow their own stubborn desires, living according to their own ideas.*[53] A note in my Bible about this verse says, "Thus for God to abandon his people to their sins is the most fearful of punishments."[54] I think each of us can recognize a time in our lives when we would say amen to that statement. Keeping in mind that God's punishment is perfect enables us to look for ways that we "let the chips fall as they may," or we allow the consequences of our children's disobedience to be the punishment.

So how do we take these concepts into the discipline and punishment of our children?

- Make sure that your children understand what behavior you expect. I find kids much more compliant to right behavior when it has been explained to them ahead of time. It only takes a moment to say, "We are going to visit Aunt Joan for a few minutes. Can you sit quietly in your chairs and use your inside voices while we're there? And remember, if she offers a plate of cookies, no more than two!"

- In many instances, it is appropriate to tell your children ahead of time what the consequences of disobedience will be. For instance, you might say, "Remember that we're planning to go to the park after we visit Aunt Joan. If you misbehave, we will have to go straight home without the park." Do not bind yourself to always explaining the consequences in advance, because unexpected disobediences will arise.

- Be sure that punishment is doable. It would be difficult to ground one child if the whole family planned to go to the park.

- Be sure the punishment is indeed punishment to that child. I had a child who loved to go to her room and read. Sending her into isolation did little good. Today, children often have too many fun things in their room for that to be a place of punishment.

- See if there is a way to allow the child to rectify the damage done by his disobedience. In the example of visiting Aunt Joan, your child could write a note of apology to her for any misbehavior. As another example, if your child pokes his finger in his brother's dessert, he will have to trade desserts—even if his brother's is half-eaten.

- Deliver punishment with a calm, matter-of-fact tone.

Remember that you are the adult in charge. No anger is needed on your part. Your discipline and punishment is far more effective if your emotions are under control.

- Except when danger is involved, do not rescue your children from their disobedience.
- Wait a little while to administer discipline. That time allows you to think with less emotion and your child to fidget.
- Keep in mind that the long-range goal of discipline and punishment is to bring your children to that important moment when they step into adulthood, ready to handle life on their own.

Appendix E:
Volunteer Opportunities for Kids

Serving others together as a family is a life-changing experience. I once stood in line with a group of kids and adults waiting to order burgers. They were returning from a week in New Mexico, serving on an Indian reservation.

A teen girl told me, "I'm about to get my driver's license. I've been bugging my daddy about the kind of car he'd buy me. Now I realize I'm just blessed to have a dad buy me a car—any kind of car. When I get home, I'm telling him how much I appreciate him, and I'll be happy with whatever he wants to get for me."

Volunteering does that for all of us. Our perspective changes so what we once thought was a big deal is no longer that important. And little things like family and home become big things.

Below are a few resources to help you find places to volunteer with your children. Of course, your research in your own community will uncover many needs.

Happy Volunteering!

- Kids of Courage:
  http://www.kidsofcourage.com/?page_id=8967
- Birthday Blessings:
  http://www.birthdayblessingministries.org/

- Samaritan's Purse:
  http://www.samaritanspurse.org/operation-christmas-child/volunteer-with-occ/
- Compassion:
  http://www.compassion.com/kids-magazine.htm
- Raised to Action: http://raisedtoaction.com/
- Adopt a shut-in in your community. You can shop for groceries, change light bulbs, or listen. This is a great opportunity for your children to be a friend to an older or disabled person—someone different from them.

Endnotes

1 Dr. Seuss, *Horton and the Kwuggerbug and More Lost Stories* (New York: Random House Children's Books, 2014)

2 Carole A. Bell, "Laughing Together," (*Parenting from the Source,* November 29, 2011)
http://www.parentingfromthesource.com/laughing-together/

3 Frank Ball, "Elsie's Night Out."
http://www.frankball.org/elsies-night-out/

4 Matthew 18:12–14

5 Lakeshore Learning, *Draw & Write Journal* (Lakeshore Learning)
http//:www.lakeshorelearning.com

6 Crystal Bowman, *The One Year Devotions for Preschoolers* (Carol Stream, IL: Tyndale House Publishers, 2004)

7 Gwen Ellis, *Read and Share Devotional* (Nashville, TN: Tommy Nelson, A Division of Thomas Nelson, 2008)

8 Young, Sarah, *Jesus Calling Story Book,* (Nashville, TN: Tommy Nelson, A Division of Thomas Nelson, 2012)

9 *NIrV Study Bible for Kids* (Grand Rapids, MI: Zonderkidz, 2015)

10 John Trent and Kurt Bruner, *Spiritual Growth of Children* (Bemidji, MN: Focus Publishing, 2003)

[11] John R.Kohlenberger, III, Ed., *Zondervan NIV Nave's Topical Bible,* (Grand Rapids, MI: Zondervan Publishing House, 1994) .

[12] "Though economists have long argued the contrary, a growing body of evidence suggests that, at our core, both animals and human beings have what Dacher Keltner at the University of California, Berkeley, coins a 'compassionate instinct.' In other words, compassion is a natural and automatic response that has ensured our survival. Research by Jean Decety, at the University of Chicago, showed that even rats are driven to empathize with another suffering rat and to go out of their way to help it out of its quandary. Studies with chimpanzees and human infants too young to have learned the rules of politeness, also back up these claims. Michael Tomasello and other scientists at the Max Planck Institute, in Germany, have found that infants and chimpanzees spontaneously engage in helpful behavior and will even overcome obstacles to do so. They apparently do so from intrinsic motivation without expectation of reward." Read the entire article at: https://www.psychologytoday.com/blog/feeling-it/201306/ compassion-our-first-instinct

[13] Matthew 25:34–40

[14] On loving ourselves as a prerequisite to loving others: "And you must love the Lord your God with all your heart, all your soul, all your mind, and all your strength. The second is equally important: 'Love your neighbor as yourself.' No other commandment is greater than these." (Mark 12:30–31)

[15] Max Lucado, *You Are Special* (Wheaton, IL, Crossway Books, A Division of Good News Publishers, 1997)

[16] Max Lucado, *If Only I Had a Green Nose* (Wheaton, IL, Crossway Books, A Division of Good News Publishers, 2002)

[17] Mark 12:31

[18] Selina Hastings, *The Children's Illustrated Bible (New York*: DK Publishing, Inc., 2005) 118-119.

[19] I Samuel 17:32–50

[20] I Samuel 17:45 (NIrV)

[21] 2 Timothy 1:7 (NIrV)

[22] Genesis 1:28 (NKJV)

[23] Luke 12:48

[24] Genesis 128 (NKJV)

[25] Psalm 50:9–10

[26] Mary Ann Spencer Pulaski, PhD. *Understanding Piaget: An Introduction to Children's Cognitive Development,* (New York: Harper and Row Publishers, 1980). Many parents will find the entire book enlightening, but a summary of the stages of cognitive development is found on pages 214–217.

[27] Acts 4:32 NIrV

[28] Psalm 24:1–2

[29] Matthew 22:36-40

[30] Brett and Kate McKay, "Creating a Positive Family Culture: How and Why to Create a Family Mission Statement," (The Art of Manliness, August 21, 2013) http://www.artofmanliness.com/2013/08/21/creating-a-family-culture-how-and-why-to-create-a-family-mission-statement/

[31] Sheila Seifert and Jeanne Gowen Dennis, "Writing a Family Mission Statement," (Focus on the Family 2013) http://www.focusonthefamily.com/parenting/spiritual-growth-for-kids/writing-a-family-mission-statement

[32] Wooden, John, *A Lifetime of Observations and Reflections on and off the Court,* (New York: McGraw Hill, 1997), 199.

[33] Marc, Weissbluth, M.D., *Healthy Sleep Habits, Healthy Child,* (New York: Ballentine Books, 2003)

[34] Sears, William, M.D. http://www.askdrsears.com/

[35] The Scholastic Store, "12 Ways to Develop Your Child's Organizational Skills." (Parents Raising Readers and Learners)

http://www.scholastic.com/parents/resources/article/social-emotional-skills/12-ways-to-develop-your-childs-organizational-skills

[36] Merrill, Susan, Dir., "Ten Social Manners for Kids," (iMOM) http://www.imom.com/printable/10-social-manners-for-kids/#.VkUUtfmrShc

[37] Carol McD. Wallace, *Elbows off the Table, Napkin in the Lap, No Video Games during Dinner, The Modern Guide to Teaching Children Good Manner* (New York: St Martin's Press) 1996.

[38] Peggy Post and Cindy Post Senning, *The Gift of Good Manners: A Parent's Guide to Raising Respectful, Kind, Considerate Children,* (New York: HarperResource, An Imprint of HarperCollins Publishers, Inc. 2002).

[39] Emily Post, *Etiquette in Society, in Business, in Politics, and at Home* (New York: Funk & Wagnalls, 1922) quoted in Elizabeth L. Post, *Emily Post's Etiquette, A guide to Modern Manners, 14th Edition,* (New York:1984: Harper and Row Publisher, Inc., 1984) xiii.

[40] Colossians 3:23

[41] Dollie Freeman, "7 Household Chores for Toddlers and Pre-schoolers," (Teachers of Good Things) http://www.joyinthehome.com/7-household-chores-for-toddlers-and-preschoolers/

[42] Carole A. Bell, L.P.C., "Chores: 3 Answers to the Question— Should Kids Be Paid, (Parenting from the Source, June 6, 2012) http://www.parentingfromthesource.com/chores-3-answers-to-the-question-should-kids-be-paid/

[43] Carole A. Bell, L.P.C., "Chores: Establish 2 Pay Grades for Your Kids," (Parenting from the Source, June 8, 2012) http://www.parentingfromthesource.com/chores-establish-2-pay-grades-for-your-kids/

[44] Mayo Clinic Staff, "Solid Food: How to Get Your Baby Started," MayoClinic.org, http://www.mayoclinic.org/healthy-lifestyle/

infant-and-toddler-health/in-depth/healthy-baby/art-20046200?pg=2

[45] Meghan Holohan, "Many Packaged Baby Foods Exceed Limits of These Foods, (Today Parents, June 9, 2015) http://www.today.com/parents/packaged-food-babies-toddlers-loaded-sugar-salt-t14121

[46] 1 Corinthians 6:19

[47] Job 38:4-7 NKJV

[48] 1 Corinthians 6:19–20

[49] Butler, Katy, "The Grim Neurology of Teenage Drinking," (New York: The New York Times, July 4, 2006). http://www.nytimes.com/2006/07/04/health/04teen.html?pagewanted=all&_r=0

[50] Dorothy Sayers, *The Lost Tools of Learning,* A speech delivered in 1947 at Oxford University, Electronic Edition, (The Fig Classic Series, 2011)

[51] Carole A. Bell, L.P.C., "Chores: 5 ways to Get Organized" *Parenting from the Source* (ParentingfromtheSource.com, May 30, 1912). http://www.parentingfromthesource.com/chores-5-ways-to-get-organized/#sthash.dqwGNx3S.dpuf

[52] Carole A. Bell, L.P.C., "Chores: 5 ways to Get Organized" *Parenting from the Source* (ParentingfromtheSource.com, May 30, 1912). http://www.parentingfromthesource.com/chores-5-ways-to-get-organized/#sthash.dqwGNx3S.dpuf

[53] Psalm 81:12

[54] Barker, Kenneth L., "Psalm 81:12" footnote" Zondervan NIV Study Bible (Grand Rapids, MI: Zondervan, 2008) 880.

54355164R00133

Made in the USA
Charleston, SC
02 April 2016